# Reclaiming
# Friendship

Foreword by Edgar Metzler

# Reclaiming Friendship

## Relating to Each Other in a Frenzied World

# Ajith Fernando

HERALD PRESS
Scottdale, Pennsylvania
Waterloo, Ontario

**Library of Congress Cataloging-in-Publication Data**
Fernando, Ajith.
    Reclaiming friendship : relating to each other in a frenzied
world / Ajith Fernando ; foreword by Edgar Metzler.
       p. cm.
    Includes bibliographical references.
    ISBN 0-8361-3630-6
    1. Friendship—Religious aspects—Christianity.
2. Interpersonal relations—Religious aspects—Christianity. I. Title.
BV4647.F7F47  1993
241'.676—dc20                                   92-37250
                                             CIP

The paper used in this publication is recycled and meets the minimum requirements of American National Standard for Information Sciences—
Permanence of Paper for Printed Library Materials, ANSI Z39.48-1984.

All Bible quotations are used by permission, all rights reserved and unless
otherwise indicated are taken from the *Holy Bible: New International Version.*
Copyright © 1973, 1978, 1984 International Bible Society; RSV, from the
Revised Standard Version of the Bible, copyright 1946, 1952, 1971 by the
Division of Christian Education of the National Council of the Churches of
Christ in the USA; NEB, from *The New English Bible* © The Delegates of the
Oxford University Press and the Syndics of the Cambridge University
Press 1961, 1970.

*To*
*My Colleagues*

*Brian and Parames Blacker*
*Richard and Dawn Brohier*
*Adrian and Ophelia De Visser*
*Tony and Cal Senewiratne*
*Suri and Shanthi Williams*

*With Gratitude*
*for Friendship*

# Contents

Spiritual accountability versus superficial
   fellowship
Warmth in times of need
Strength to defend ourselves
Friendship and personal problems
The pleasantness of friends

# Foreword

**F**riendship has been the subject of many articles and books in recent years. In the publications that cross the desk of my wife, a psychotherapist, I see numerous references to the topic. Friendship may seem an obvious and simple reality we can take for granted.

But for many, friendship involves nearly insurmountable problems that must be addressed. Why? My hunch is that the attention to friendship reflects much more than the professional curiosity of social scientists and counselors. It is probably rooted in the tension between our inherent need for friendship and frustration of that need by our culture.

Created by God, we are born into relationships and destined to fulfill our potential in and through relationships. The biblical image of the divine, in which we are created, includes the relationships between Father, Son, and Holy Spirit. Some theologians have suggested that the doctrine of the Trinity reflects God's own need for friendship and relationship!

Our search for the friendships we need, however, has been complicated by the shift in Western society (since the industrial revolution) from family and local communities to larger, more impersonal organizations. This has affected the nature of relationships in the realms of work, politics, education, the church, and more.

Christians recognize that longing for friendship expresses our soul's desire to become what our Creator intends us to be. From such a perspective, it might be assumed that Christians, committed to Jesus as the way to realize God's intention for them, have no problems with friendship.

This is not the case, of course. Christians are affected by cultural obstacles to friendship. And Christian discipleship is a process of growth. Developing significant relationships is part of that challenge.

Anyone who wants to take up that challenge will find Ajith Fernando a stimulating and practical guide. The wisdom literature of the Bible, particularly Proverbs and Ecclesiastes, provides his starting point.

The author writes from an Asian perspective, but he knows the West well, especially the organizational culture of churches and parachurch groups. Those of us from the West who have been privileged to work in Asia have learned to appreciate the importance given to friendship by Asians.

The cultural priority of time for nurturing relationships is sometimes frustrating to Westerners preoccupied with "getting things done." But Fernando argues that learning to linger is essential for friendship.

The author sees biblical friendship as rooted in Christian community. The image of the church as the body of Christ pervades the book. The resulting "body theology," applied in very specific examples and suggestions, views the church as a community of friends. Team members are not only co-workers but friends. Through the lens of friendship, marriage and family relationships are also seen in fresh ways.

Many of us experience life as more impersonal than did our grandparents. Many of us complain that there simply is not enough time for friendships. The demands of earning a living, creating and maintaining a home, fulfilling church and job responsibilities, and other time pressures make deep relationships seem a luxury.

No! exclaims Ajith Fernando. Far from a luxury, relationships are an absolute necessity. In *Reclaiming Friendship* he guides us in fulfilling the need for friendship placed in us by our Creator.

*—Edgar Metzler, Executive Director*
*United Mission to Nepal*
*Kathmandu, Nepal*
*First Sunday of Advent 1992*

# *Author's Preface*

**M**uch of the work on this book was done while I was on writing sabbatical at Gordon-Conwell Theological Seminary (Mass.), preparing a book on the doctrine of eternal punishment. Early in the sabbatical I spoke on team ministry at a leadership seminar held at the seminary and organized by Leighton Ford and Bob Reccord. I was surprised by the positive response to this talk.

A series of Bible expositions I did at an "East Coast Ingathering" organized by Jews for Jesus gave me further opportunity to reflect on friendship. The organizers asked me to offer teaching on personal relationships based on the book of Proverbs. Preparing longer series of messages for the staff of British Youth for Christ helped me delve further into the material. Since returning to Sri Lanka, I have taught this material to many Christians mostly in Youth for Christ.

During my sabbatical, my first extended stay in the West since my student days in the 1970s, I was gripped by growing concern about models of community life some Christian groups had adopted. I believed these models violated the biblical teaching about how the body of Christ should operate.

Christian views of friendship and interpersonal relationships are dangerously influenced by the values of the world. As a result Christians are missing the enrichment God intended them to get from friendship. I see that the groups with which they are connected hurt many Christians. This has added a sense of urgency to my work on this book.

I received much stimulation from an international study commission of Youth for Christ which dealt with human resource development and arrived at conclusions similar to those described in this book. What you have here is actually a study of Christian community life, a key feature of which is relationships of accountability—to which we have given the name *friendships.*

In this book you will read many references to the way the world has adversely influenced the church. You may get the impression that I am on a tirade against modern Western management systems. I am not. In fact, I am not qualified to critique these systems. I am, however, responding to what I have seen in Christian groups. I find that systems which I know to be common in business organizations, but which have no place in Christian groups, have crept into many Christian gatherings.

When I described the concerns I bring up in this

book to friends more conversant with modern management literature than I, they told me my own concerns are also being expressed in recent secular management books. That does not surprise me. After all, the systems of management recommended by the Creator of the world should have much in common with systems recommended by wise people in this same world God created.

As I proceeded with my study of Proverbs, I realized the book contained antidotes to many of the problems I saw with friendships. So I decided to share through this book what I had learned.

Today many people in search of what they call "self-fulfillment" believe costly commitment to others is unneeded and bothersome. But costly commitment yields the self-fulfillment that really matters. God has chosen to give some of his richest blessings to us through our loving service and commitment to others.

It is appropriate that I dedicate a book on friendship to my five senior colleagues in Sri Lanka Youth for Christ and their wives. They have long been my team members in ministry. Two are no longer on staff with us. But their friendship and support continue.

The contribution of these, my friends, to my growth as a Christian and minister cannot be adequately described. They have taught me much of what I know about ministry. It has been my privilege to share with a larger audience, through writing, what we have together learned as a ministering community. So in a sense this book shares scriptural principles of community life we have experienced together.

In recent times our staff team has realized afresh

how crucial is a close community life as we seek to serve Christ in a land torn by violence and strife. Yet much of our learning has been the result of mistakes we have made. Our experience of community life has not been without its fair share of serious problems.

I must also mention the community of the Nugegoda Methodist Church. My wife and I have served on the leadership team there for the past decade. Our lives have been greatly enriched through that experience.

I am grateful to Christy and Betty Wilson, Gary and Norma Bekker, Nairy Ohanian, and Peter and Louise Burton from the community at Gordon-Conwell Theological Seminary. They became our friends and helped me and my family in so many ways when we were "strangers in a strange land."

This is the first book I have written on a computer. The computer made it so much easier to develop the original expositions into a book. I am grateful to Jack and Lisa Alexander, who gave me a computer without ever having met me, based on an appeal from their friend and mine, Jayson Kyle.

A preface to a book on friendship requires reference to my best friend and companion in life, Nelun, and our children, Nirmali and Asiri. They brought me so much brightness as I tried to teach a class, write two books, and work on checking a new translation of the Sinhala Bible—all on a six-month sabbatical!

I have written this book for Christians seeking to read a devotional book. The form is thus expositional. The material is also suited for group study. I have tried to write at a level accessible to lay persons yet still helpful to persons active in Christian ministry. In the appendix I have included material particularly applicable to leaders and full-time Christian workers.

In addition to passages from Proverbs, I decided to use the famous text on friendship from the next book in the Bible, Ecclesiastes, which like Proverbs belongs to the wisdom literature. Yet this book should not be viewed as an exhaustive study of such Bible books. What I have tried to do is examine texts in Proverbs and Ecclesiastes and glean insights from them about friendship. My goal has then been to apply these insights to our contemporary experience.

I need to express my indebtedness to the commentaries of Proverbs that were always by my side as I wrote. Especially helpful were commentaries by Kenneth Aitken, Robert Alden, Charles Bridges, Derek Kidner, and Charles Martin. Stephen Voorwinde's *Wisdom for Today's Issues,* a topical arrangement of the Proverbs, was also very helpful. I came across Gary Inrig's fine book, *Quality Friendship,* only as I was coming to the end of my writing. Inrig offers many good insights into biblical teaching about friendship.

I send this book out with the prayer that it will help many Christians resist the contemporary cultural trend away from establishing lasting and committed ties with others. I pray many will be encouraged to form close Christian friendships and experience the enrichment God intended friendships to offer us.

—*Ajith Fernando*
*Colombo, Sri Lanka*

# Reclaiming Friendship

# ONE

# *Friends and Real Friends*

**W**hen I was in my late teens and early twenties, I belonged to a small group of Youth for Christ volunteers who met regularly for fellowship, usually on Sunday nights. We would talk for hours about issues related to our lives and ministry. We shared our problems and joys, we discussed, we debated, and we prayed.

Some members of that original group are still active in Youth for Christ. Others are active in churches and other organizations. But when we meet it does not take us long to experience again the joy of Christian friendship. During our early times together, ties based on truth had developed. Such ties do not dissolve during years of separation, unless we reject the truth that was the foundation of the friendship.

This is quite a contrast to some friendships I had as

a schoolboy. These too were close friendships—but only for a time. When I meet old school friends now, I am usually happy. But after some time there isn't much to talk about. Those were temporary friendships because they were based on things that did not last.

My experiences with the Youth for Christ volunteers in those crucial years of my spiritual growth remind me of an incident from John Wesley's early life, recorded in his journal. He once met a person whom he calls a "serious man." The man told Wesley, "Sir, you wish to serve God and go to heaven? Remember that you cannot serve him alone. You must therefore find companions or make them. The Bible knows nothing of solitary religion." Wesley never forgot that wise counsel. Much later he said, "Christianity is a social religion. To turn it into a solitary religion is indeed to destroy it."

A great contribution of the early Methodist movement was to bring back to the church the practice of spiritual accountability found in the early church. The recent rise of individualism in the church requires renewed emphasis on this biblical understanding of community life. I hope to offer such emphasis in this book. We will take principles concerning friendship from the Bible and see how they apply today. We begin with an important affirmation about the nature of friendship found in Proverbs.

## Two Types of Friends
Proverbs 18:24 speaks of two types of friends. It says, "A man of many companions may come to ruin, but there is a friend who sticks closer than a brother." The

form of this proverb is typical of Hebrew poetry, which usually has two statements related to each other in some way. This is called parallelism. In this verse the two statements give converse truths.

The first line has been understood in various ways. The rendering in the King James, "A man that has friends must show himself friendly," is probably wrong. The basic idea is probably that there are two types of friends. The various translations give the sense of what the first group is like. The New International Version (NIV) renders it, "A man of many companions may come to ruin." Here the emphasis is on how dangerous this type of friendship is. The Revised Standard Version (RSV) rendering clarifies the danger: "There are friends who pretend to be friends." Whatever the exact meaning, this line points to the fact that we could have acquaintances who are not real friends.

The second statement in this couplet describes "a friend who sticks closer than a brother." The word translated *sticks* is the same word used of a husband cleaving to his wife (Gen. 2:24), of Ruth clinging to her mother-in-law Naomi (Ruth 1:14) and of Israel cleaving to the Lord (Deut. 10:20; 11:22). According to the *Theological Wordbook of the Old Testament*, "sticks" has the sense of clinging to someone in affection and loyalty (p. 178). These two ideas of affection and loyalty are the key to true friendship and the rest of Proverbs expounds this.

The use of the figure of *brother* in comparing the value of friendship is significant. Many converts to Christianity have endured alienation from family members because they became Christians. We must never give up trying to mend these family relationships. Indeed, if we continue to show love and loyalty to the family despite rejection, after some time relationships may be restored.

But in the meantime, God compensates—first by his comforting presence, then through the friendship of fellow Christians. And as Proverbs 18:24 tells us, the closeness of these friends could be more intimate even than our closeness to family members, for such friends stick closer than a brother.

Thus there are two types of friends—friends and *real* friends. Derek Kidner says that "Proverbs . . . is emphatic that a few close friends are better than a host of acquaintances, and stand in a class by themselves." Even Jesus showed this. He ministered to the crowds, but he had a group of special friends, the twelve disciples. From among the twelve Jesus chose the inner circle of three and from them the "disciple whom Jesus loved."

## Friends Versus Cliques

But Jesus was not cliquish. Cliques form when people are friendly purely for selfish reasons. Because of the selfish motivation behind the friendship, cliques often cut themselves off from others they see as a threat. Cliques reject others, speak ill of others, and gossip about them.

On the other hand, the small group Jesus had was a ministering community. The community's mission was to serve people. Receiving strength from the fellowship, community members ministered sacrificially to people's needs. So we are not advocating a clique. Cliques alienate people. Biblical friendships serve people.

To those involved in ministry, I might mention that we must seek to dispel the misconception that we are only concerned about our "close friends." This is a criticism often leveled against those who practice intimate community life. One way of dealing with the criticism is to abstain at public gatherings from talking only with these close friends. These are public events and are best used as an opportunity to become better friends with persons we do not know well.

We should let others in the congregation or whatever group we lead know that those closest to us, our team members, have joined us to help in service and are willing to pay the price of commitment required by such people. They are our team, not our clique.

## *Alien to Our Culture*

Our cultural environment is not conducive to the close relationships Proverbs advocates. People are friendly today—friendly with a lot of people! But when you are a friend of many, you may end up being the close friend of nobody.

We get so used to small talk that it becomes a strain to work at serious and honest talk. Besides, ours is a generation of busybodies. We enjoy going from place to place, keeping active all the time. Busybodies find it a strain to concentrate when others are pouring out their hearts. When the sharers realize this, they stop sharing. By our inability to make time to listen, we make it impossible for close friendships to develop.

We will show in a later chapter that the idea of lasting commitments have also gone out of fashion. This then has eroded the possibility of true friendship, which requires commitment.

*Friendship and Truth.* One key to a deep friendship is time spent in long conversations. As the gospels show, this is the type of relationship Jesus had with his friends, the disciples. Jesus said, "I have called you friends, for everything that I learned from my Father I have made known to you" (John 15.15). At the heart of such friendship was communication of truth.

Proverbs may not expressly state the value of extended conversations but it does imply it. This is how the company of the wise (which we will describe below) can operate. This is how the wisdom that comes from friends (the topic of chapter 6) is mediated.

Many people don't seem to have time for long conversations. They have so many things to do! When they have free time, it is spent on entertainment. So leisure time is packed with trips to the beach, vacations, and the like. Even when with friends, such people want to be active, to go somewhere, to play a game, to watch a movie.

We can't bear the thought of just sitting and discussing issues. If we need information, we can get it from an encyclopedia or a book. Speed-reading techniques allow us to read quickly. This is a faster way to get facts than long discussions, which are so time consuming. So the conversations we have are often confined to pragmatic issues. We talk about a decision which has to be made or entertaining topics like humor, sports, or hot current events.

The problem with all this is that we are simply getting facts into our minds. We are not interacting with the facts. We are not asking what we will do with what we read. We are producing technicians with a lot of facts, rather than thinkers.

Thinkers have depth. And depth has a richness to it. It satisfies the deep desire in our hearts implanted by a God who is committed to truth. God's understanding of truth includes more than facts. Christian truth has a qualitative and experiential aspect to it. So truth can be enjoyed only if we are willing to linger with it, to ask what its implications are, to ask how it should influence our thinking and acting. Is it any wonder our generation does not know the joy of truth about which the Psalms speak so much?

Those who set apart time for enriching discussions on issues, on the things of God, will rediscover the joy of truth. They will bring new depth of true personal fulfillment to their lives. We need to bring long chats back into our schedules, allowing significant slots of time for truth-related discussions. Truth is one of the richest aspects of the Christian life and so should be one of the richest aspects of Christian fellowship.

Proverbs 15:31 says, "He who listens to a life-giving rebuke will be at home among the wise." This verse implies that there is such a thing as a fellowship of wise people—people committed to the pursuit of knowledge. That is what we are advocating in this book. We are asking that friendships be characterized by the quest for a deeper understanding of truth.

I have found that truth-seeking dialogues cause many scheduling inconveniences. Most are not previously planned. They simply emerge during an ordinary conversation. But that inconvenience is a price worth paying, for through these conversations I receive knowledge which refreshes and enriches me. As Proverbs 2:10 says, "Wisdom will enter your heart, and knowledge will be pleasant to your soul."

Anyone who takes the call of Christ seriously will soon encounter a basically selfish approach to life that is prevalent today but is contrary to the Christian way. Such a person will find it encouraging to meet others who also follow the path of discipleship.

The presence of common convictions amidst the confusion of today's world is an important ingredient of Christian friendship. As C. S. Lewis puts it, "Friendship . . . is born at the moment when one says to another 'What! you too? I thought that no one but myself. . . .' " (p. 92). Being among others who seem to understand gives people the courage to persevere along their chosen path of nonconformity.

We are not advocating a club of intellectual snobs who think that because they belong to the company of the wise they are superior. The key to entering this company is teachability. Proverbs 15:31 says that it is the one "who listens to a life-giving rebuke" who "will be at home with the wise." Intellectual snobs are always trying to show how wise they are. Such cannot have true fellowship. Those belonging to the fellowship of wise people want to learn from each other. So intense is their desire to do this that they are open to rebuke from others.

This is the type of relationship the Old Testament advocates that parents have with their children. Parents should talk with their children about truth. They are the first to teach children the basics of the faith. The fathers have a big part to play in this (cf. Prov. 1:8-9; 4:1-6; 6:20-24).

Interesting provisions were made in Hebrew rituals for children to ask questions of their parents. For example, stones were placed as a memorial of the crossing of the Jordan, with the express purpose of provoking a question from children. This in turn provided parents with an opportunity to relate the story of God's great act (Josh. 4:1-9). An important part of the Passover ritual was when a son asked the father "How is this night different from other nights?"

Today some of the most useful times parents can have with their children are occasions for discussing issues. This is a key to developing meaningful friendships between parents and children.

Our point then is that the quest for understanding truth should be a key aspect of Christian interpersonal relationships. The activity orientation of today's society, expressed in its love affair with quick, tangible results, makes truth seeking difficult. The problem has become so serious that I heard a leading American theologian once say that it has become almost impossible for North America to develop fresh theology. He thinks the society has become so pragmatically oriented that people have trouble thinking in terms of truth categories.

The result of such pragmatism is emptiness which truth alone can fill. Those who will give time for truth-related discussions will be richly rewarded. They will find "the fullness of truth" vital for the fulfillment of human beings made in the image of the God of truth.

Christians all over the world are indebted to C. S. Lewis for the great wisdom he made available to the church through his writings. Lewis had many friends. He had what biographers call his "inner circle," made up of such friends as Arthur Greeves, Owen Barfield, J. R. R. Tolkien, Charles Williams, and his wife, Joy Davidman. George Sayer in his book *Jack: C. S. Lewis and His Times* makes it clear these people had much to do with the developing of Lewis' great insights.

Lewis included a classic statement on friendship in *The Four Loves.*

> He is lucky beyond desert to be in such company. Especially when the whole group is together, each bringing out all that is best, wisest, or funniest in all the others. Those are the golden sessions; when four or five of us after a hard day's walking have come to our inn; when our slippers are on, our feet spread out towards the blaze and our drinks at our elbows; when the whole world, and something beyond the world, opens itself to our minds as we talk; and no one has any claim on or any responsibility for another, but all are freemen and equals as if we had first met an hour ago, while at the same time an affection mellowed by the years enfolds us. Life—natural life—has no better gift to give. Who could have deserved it? (p. 85).

*The Importance of Learning to Linger.* The type of friendship we are advocating is rare today because we have forgotten how to linger. Time is too precious for lingering, we claim. Indeed time is precious. But that is not why we have stopped lingering, for lingering is a good way to spend precious time. Our problem is that we are too restless to linger.

We don't know what it is to be silent before God. We don't know what it is to meditate on truth. Similarly we don't know what it is to spend long periods of conversation with friends. It is in such times that minds meet, that we experience together the joy of truth which is one of the most precious forms of joy. People who let long conversations eat into their schedules—and that is a sacrifice—will know the joy of minds meeting on a deep level. From such depths true friendships will be forged.

Jesus was willing to sacrifice time in exchange for friendship. When Andrew and another of the disciples of John asked Jesus where he was staying, he did not simply give the information they wanted. He said, "Come and . . . see." They went "and spent that day with him" (John 1:37-39). It was about 4:00 p.m. when they went home, and it seems that these two spent the night with Christ. (See Leon Morris' book, *Reflections on the Gospel of John*, p. 77.) The Savior of the world, perfect model for the Christian leader, was inefficient according to much modern management philosophy. He spent a whole day on an unplanned appointment!

Most people today would say that they don't have time for such extended contacts with people. So friendship has become something cheap and shallow. Like many other words, friendship has lost its original meaning. Our understanding of friendship has thus been diluted. Inflation has hit not only the economic scene, but also the area of interpersonal relationships!

Take the practice of shaking hands. This seems to

have originated as the sign of a blood covenant, when a pledge would be taken that one would protect another's life. This pledge would be sealed by the clasping of hands and the shedding of blood. How far that ritual is from the meaning this practice has today!

Another evidence of the inflation that has taken place in our understanding of friendship is what we understand by the word *friendly*. To us a friendly person makes acquaintances easily. This person is usually the life and soul of a party. Such a quality is not necessarily a bad one. But often these so-called friendly people don't have many deep friends. They have many superficial acquaintances, which is not bad, but they have no close friends, which *is* bad.

## The Marriage Relationship

The problem of not having time for extended conversations has affected many husband-wife relationships. Before marriage there were dates, which provided so many opportunities for conversation. But after the wedding the couple comes back to reality and gets on with the business of living. There are so many things to do. The children take up so much energy. Where is the time for long conversations? But without deep discussion, couples grow distant. However much they love each other, they can't remain best friends unless they communicate in an extended way. And isn't that what couples are supposed to be—best friends?

My wife and I have found that the best times for us to talk are after the children have gone to bed. This may require us to stay up into the night. We are often quite tired the next day. But we're happy! Hearts have communicated, and that brings immense satisfaction. It also gives security. We live in a world where people are competing and struggling to overtake each other. It is good to know that there are some people who will accept us for what we are, and in whose presence we can let our hair down, be ourselves, and talk about things that really matter to us.

We conclude by repeating ourselves one more time. True friendship calls for *time*—time to talk.

# TWO

# Team Ministry

In the last chapter we discussed implications of the statement in Proverbs 18:24 that "there is a friend who sticks closer than a brother." We said that Jesus' relationship with his disciples was a good example of this close friendship. The relationship Jesus had with his disciples can best be described as that of a ministering team.

## New Testament Ministry Teams

There is evidence in the New Testament that team ministry is God's preferred way. Only in exceptional cases, like that of Philip the evangelist, do we see ministry being done alone in the New Testament. And even in the case of Philip we cannot be sure that he went to Samaria alone (although it seems clear that he was alone when he met the Ethiopian eunuch).

When Jesus sent out his twelve apostles for ministry, they were sent two by two (Mark 6:7). Two by two was also the pattern for the seventy-two disciples who went on a ministry tour (Luke 10:1). When Peter rose to speak on the day of Pentecost, he "stood up with the Eleven" (Acts 2:14). When he talked of his witness, he said, "*We* are witnesses of these things" (5:32; cf. 2:32; 3:15; emphasis added). He was not a lone voice, but part of the ministry team backing him as he preached. Thereafter Peter and John ministered as a team (Acts 3:1, 4; 4:1, 23; 8:14). When Peter went to the home of Cornelius on his historic visit, he took six brothers with him (Acts 10:23; 11:12).

Upon commissioning the first missionary team in the history of the church, the Holy Spirit said, "Set apart for me Barnabas and Saul"(Acts 13:2). When they separated, both Paul and Barnabas took others with them.

And we know Paul almost never traveled alone. He had his famous traveling Bible school, where he trained interns like Timothy and Titus. Even as Paul went to Rome as prisoner, Luke was with him (Acts 27:2). In his last letter written from prison, Paul told Timothy, "Do your best to come to me quickly. . . . Only Luke is with me. Get Mark and bring him with you, because he is helpful to me in my ministry" (2 Tim. 4:9, 11).

So we can safely say that in the Bible team ministry is the normal style. As we go on, we will see that this is for good reasons. We should be careful about sending a person on a ministry assignment alone, especially when we are starting a work in a new area. The pitfalls and discouragements of pioneering work are so intense that those who go to start a new work should generally go as a team.

## *Effectiveness of Teams*

Ecclesiastes 4:9-12 is perhaps the best known passage in Scripture on the value of a team. Most of the affirmations in this passage will be studied later (chapter 9). Here we will discuss only the first affirmation. Verse 9 says, "Two are better than one, because they have a good return for their work." Emphasized is the productivity of a team. When different people contribute to a project, the gifts of each are used, and the result is richer than if only one person contributed.

This is the thrust of 1 Corinthians 12, the great passage on gifts, where Paul says that Christians join to form a body in much the same way as the physical parts of a human being join to form the human body. With Christ as the head, Christians then form the body of Christ.

A common example used to describe the value of differing gifts is of a team preparing for an evangelistic rally. A gifted artist designs an attractive handbill. Committed people use the handbill when inviting friends for the program. Smiling greeters make the non-Christians who come feel welcome. Musicians present the gospel attractively. The person who shares his testimony shows what Christ can do in a person's life. The preacher faithfully proclaims the message. The counselor helps the inquirer to commit his life to Christ. And the local church provides nurture for the new Christian.

A preacher might be great, yet not be effective without the body-backing described above. A preacher with half the ability, but the backing of a team of committed people, might be highly effective.

Let me comment here on a benefit of team life not often mentioned—the way team members bring out the best in us. Our best ideas are often refined and made better when we receive input from others. Sometimes this may cause tension, but the end product is so much better. Proverbs 27:17 describes this beautifully: "As iron sharpens iron, so one man sharpens another."

Team members can best sharpen each other when they are not all alike. This seems to have been the case in the Antioch church, which had such an effective ministry of evangelism, pastoral care, relief, and missions. Acts 13:1 says, "In the church at Antioch there were prophets and teachers."

Prophets are visionaries who provide special guidance directly from the Lord for specific situations. Today, because we have a completed Bible, the prophetic gift is not so common in the church as in the first century. However, we see no convincing evidence in the Scriptures that prophecy has been taken from the church, as some claim. Though the specific gift of prophesy may be less prominent, we need prophetic voices in the church. They may not exercise the classic gift of prophecy, but their prophetic insight will direct God's people into new areas of involvement and into questioning the validity of revered traditions and practices that may not be appropriate anymore.

We can call such people "radicals," (a name which

springs from the word *root*) because they go to the roots of issues and suggest drastic changes. We need such radicals in the church. I do not refer to harmful theological radicals who deviate from the truth revealed in the Scriptures. The radicals we need are people who suggest change as they see ways the authoritative Word of God applies to specific situations.

Teachers, on the other hand, expound the Scriptures. They focus attention on the unchanging foundations of the Word of God. As their focus is on foundational principles, they are usually more conservative in their emphases.

A healthy team will include both radicals and conservatives. Usually when these two types are in the same group there is friction. The radicals struggle to have patience with the conservatives because the latter are so careful to make sure that new schemes suggested are not departures from orthodoxy. Therefore, often they give up trying to work with the team and work alone. But radicals achieve much less that way.

Conservatives often don't make an effort to understand the radicals. They either get the radicals to leave the group or they themselves leave. But their ministries also will not make much progress because there are no "ideas folk" in their group.

When radicals and conservatives work together under common commitment to the authority of Scripture, there is responsible growth. The radicals ensure growth. The conservatives ensure that the growth is responsible. The result is a team that can achieve much more than a group of people who always agree on everything.

For example visionaries, consumed with a passion to complete a task they have begun, may sometimes bend certain rules to get the job done quickly. Teachers, with their focus on principles, will object to breaking of rules and ensure that growth is responsible.

Similarly a person with a managerial orientation can help Christian groups maintain responsible growth. I have heard people criticize the accountant type of people because they are said to stifle growth and creativity. Yet I am convinced that if such people work in the context of a team, they make invaluable contributions.

We have a volunteer accountant, Chandran Williams, who as part of our leadership team manages our administrative and financial operations. At times I have excitedly gone to him for funds to purchase some piece of equipment I am sure we need for our work. Often Chandran suggests we delay making the purchase until he studies our needs and the available equipment. This taxes my patience. But how grateful I am that we waited for his wise counsel and bought what was best, not simply what I got excited about!

Sometimes we may have a leader who feels some project is urgent and tries to use funds designated for something else—promising, of course, to pay back this money sometime later. Accountants usually object to such a procedure.

Then there are certain projects which take much money to set up and maintain. Because we have raised the initial investment, we may want to launch the project. But we have not made adequate plans for raising funds needed to maintain the project. Accountants usually object to this procedure too.

Too often, caught up in the excitement of the project, we ignore these objections and go ahead. How many churches and organizations have faced serious difficulties because they did not heed the warnings of accountant types. In a team, the accountant and the visionary can harmonize to produce responsible growth that honors God.

## Friendship at Team Meetings

We are using the term *team* in a broad sense, meaning a group of people who have come together around a common goal. *Team* is a term which may be used for the different groups in a church or an organization. Examples are persons involved in a ministry project like the youth fellowship committee or the board, the team of staff workers, and the senior leaders.

We have said that these teams need to be groups where people practice the Christian art of friendship. But while ministering to others, there is usually not much opportunity to minister to team members through friendship. While doing their ministry, team members should concentrate on those they minister to, not each other. Otherwise the team will become a clique. So team meetings should be the times to express team friendship.

Such meetings usually are times when the team gathers to evaluate, plan, and discuss problems—that is, to discuss business. But this business is Christian ministry. Such business must use the Christian model of ministry. This is the *body life model*. I fear most Christian board and team meetings follow a secular business model. (I say a *secular* business model because some businesses use models compatible with the Christian model).

When shaped by the secular model, a meeting commences with the ritual opening prayer and closes with the benediction. Once in a while the business is punctuated by a testimony or a ministry report. The rest of the time, however, Robert's *Rules of Order* are more influential than the Bible in directing the style of the meeting (though we hope not the substance discussed).

The key to the body life model is the spiritual union that the members have first with Christ and through Christ with each other. A key expression of this spiritual union is "being of one mind." This idea is well expressed in the numerous times the Greek word *homothumadon* appears in the book of Acts to describe the life of the early church. This word has been translated in numerous ways, such as "of one mind," "of one accord," and "as one man." (NIV's "together" is appropriate in some instances but is usually too weak a translation.)

*Homothumadon* describes a group of people knit together by a common purpose. Sometimes the word describes people who are together in a common commitment to Christ (Acts 1:14; 2:46; 4:24; 5:12; cf. Rom. 15:6). Sometimes the word describes the way opponents of the gospel get together to battle the church (Acts 7:57; 18:12; 19:29). A uniting passion is the idea in such instances.

Such bonding is not easy, especially when the group consists of leaders with strong feelings about ways things should be done. Often a uniting passion emerges from an atmosphere of worship and frankness. The worship helps us affirm the basis of the unity, which is our common link with Christ. The frankness helps us to maintain the unity in experience. But when leaders are frank, sparks fly. The discussion sometimes grows heated as all persons share their passions.

I have been part of the Youth for Christ leadership team for a quarter-century. During these years we have had much friction, sometimes even resulting in tears. Yet all our "love fights" have ended in resolution, though sometimes the resolution took time to emerge. After the resolution has come and we have prayed together, we sense we have grown deeper in our love for and understanding of each other than before the battle.

In fact, the battle often starts because we have drifted apart. Often the drifting occurred because we had not met each other as we should have due to heavy schedules. The battle is a way God gets us back together.

The situation becomes more complex if some at the meeting are not in full fellowship with each other. Body theology demands that issues causing trouble be resolved before biblical ministry is done. Considerable time must be given for a love fight aimed at resolving the differences. But the unity forged after the resolution is deep and the ensuing ministry of this team is spiritually powerful. In fact, the meeting may proceed rapidly after the correct spiritual climate has been created, because the group is now in tune with God and itself.

Are our board meetings and team meetings structurally able to accommodate love fights? Often not. Let me give an example. The chairperson has invited a rich donor to attend the meeting as an observer. Staff persons do not feel free to be frank in the donor's presence. But the donor is impressed by the program the team is planning and makes a large donation. There is great rejoicing; the decision to invite the donor is seen to have been wise.

An impressive program is launched using the donated money. But the program is administered by a team that is not of one accord. There are impressive statistics to show the way the money was used. But the program has made little contribution to the growth of the kingdom of God. The buildings bought with the money or the materials produced are not recorded in the annals of the eternal kingdom.

The work was done "in the flesh." The work lacked God's blessing because it sidestepped God's requirements for effective service. People mistakenly assumed that the models effective in producing temporal success would also produce eternal success.

A scandal in the life of the church today is the high input of human resources, time, and money that has produced minimal impact from the perspective of eternity. This is because the work was not done in God's way.

I am not advocating meetings that drag on with different people rambling about things of no relevance to the meeting. Team members in the body life model are *homothumadon* people. They are fired by a unifying passion to achieve goals for the kingdom. Passionate people will not tolerate rambling. Their urgency will cause them to challenge all unnecessary conversation so they can give themselves to the task at hand.

Our plea then is for Christian groups to return to the body life model of ministry. It may result in what is seen as inefficient use of meeting time. But if we free ourselves from this bondage to time, which produces technical excellence without depth and the power of spiritual penetration, we will realize that most important is not the volume of work we do, but the amount of lasting impact we make.

An implication of what we have said above is that we must foster unanimity in the team concerning a given project. While this may not be directly implied in a text from Proverbs, it is certainly implied in the Acts of the Apostles. In fact, unanimity is the essential meaning of the word *homothumadon* (see *The New International Dictionary of New Testament Theology*, pp. 908-909).

The use of *homothumadon* to indicate unanimity in connection with meetings is seen in Acts 15:25: "So we all agreed to choose some men and send them to you." At the end of the controversial Jerusalem conference, those attending were unanimous about the choice of the team of people who were to take the letter from the conference to the Gentile churches. There had been much debate, but at the end unanimity was achieved.

Today we do not approach differences of opinion at meetings in this way. We don't have time for debates at team meetings. We are not used to being frank with each other, and thus disagreement is awkward. So sometimes we opt for taking a vote. Then the majority prevails.

Other times we say something like "I don't agree with this plan of yours. But that's your business. So you go ahead and do it." That may sound generous, but there is no *homothumadon* oneness in the team. So what we may call "body power" will be lacking from the project. The dissenters will not back their colleague with all their hearts. When the project goes through hard times, as most projects do, the dissenters' lack of enthusiasm will cause others (who are struggling with discouragement over problems being faced) to lose motivation.

If the project goes wrong, the dissenters will say, "We thought as much." But by refusing to explain their concerns in the decision-making process, the dissenters have hurt the body. Their approach may have helped the body make a decision quickly, but they have hurt this body in the process.

Some keep quiet so there will be peace. The fear of causing what we may call "constructive unrest" comes from lack of commitment to the body and from spiritual lethargy. It must be condemned.

The project would have been carried out with so much more spiritual power if the whole team had been of one mind. It takes time to achieve such oneness. Yet that is the price we must pay to have the power of the Holy Spirit in our ministries.

## Colleagues as Friends

A trend today is for people to have their close and warm friendships outside their ministering team or group of colleagues. Some people have their most satisfying experiences of fellowship at weekend retreats where they meet with relative strangers and share openly, warmly, and vulnerably.

It is indeed essential that Christians have good friends outside the group with which they are affiliated. This outside perspective can offer enrichment. Outside friendships express commitment to the total body of Christ, which encompasses the whole church. But outside friendships must never be a substitute for close friendships with colleagues.

Often people separate the joy of fellowship from the responsibility of ongoing commitment to those with whom they live and work closely. So their fellowship group is not the group they work with. They think it too cumbersome to have fellowship-type relationships with co-workers. But this is unnatural and distant from the fellowship model in Christ's team of disciples as well as Paul's teams as described in Acts.

Besides, those we are close to are those who can best help us grow. They know us best and can help us in an ongoing way as we go through our day-to-day lives. It is sometimes uncomfortable to live with such helpers, but it is much more effective as an agent for good in our lives.

## Leaders as Friends

When I first taught the material that ultimately became this book, one question asked of me was whether leaders can have the type of friendship I was talking about with those they lead. This becomes a particularly important issue because leaders are often told today that they must not have close relationships with followers.

A friend of mine who is a leader in a Christian organization was reprimanded by his director for being too friendly with those working under him. The reason the director gave my friend was that managers should remain distant from underlings. This seems to be an area where the world has unduly influenced the church.

The testimony of Scripture is that the great biblical leaders were open to intimate friendships with those they led. Jesus is the supreme example of leadership for the Christian. But his relationship with his disciples is also the supreme example of the value of the friendship of leaders with those led. John 15:15 is the classic statement about this. Jesus tells his disciples, "I no longer call you servants, because a servant does not know his master's business. Instead, I have called you friends, for everything that I learned from my Father I have made known to you." So Jesus related to his disciples as he would to friends.

Paul also led the young Timothy while maintaining an intimate friendship with him. Paul did not hesitate to be open about himself before Timothy. Paul told Timothy, "You, however, know all about my teaching, my way of life, my purpose, faith, patience, love, endurance, persecutions, sufferings" (2 Tim. 3:10-11). Timothy knew everything about Paul. Far from keeping his distance, Paul unashamedly expressed his feelings of affection toward Timothy. He wrote to Timothy, "I long to see you, so that I may be filled with joy" (2 Tim. 1:4).

Paul was also unashamed and unafraid to expose his emotions to the rebellious and often wayward Corinthians. He told them that even though there was an open door for preaching in Troas, he had no peace of mind until Titus came with news of how the Corinthians had received his letter (2 Cor. 2:12-13). Paul talked to them about the daily pressure of concern he had for all the churches and of how news from the churches caused strong emotional reactions in him (2 Cor. 11:28-29). Paul's classic statement in this regard is 2 Corinthians 6:11-12. "We have spoken freely to you Corinthians, and opened wide our hearts to you. We are not withholding our affection from you, but you are withholding yours from us."

In view of the above, it is not surprising that F. F. Bruce should say, in his book about Paul's friends, *The Pauline Circle*, that "Paul's genius for friendship has been spoken of so often that it has become proverbial —almost cliché." Bruce says that Paul "attracted friends around him as a magnet attracts iron filings" (pp. 8-9).

Why then is there so much reluctance today to associate friendship with leadership? One reason may be that we give too high a place to status in our understanding of leadership. As friendship seems to cause one to drop a few rungs in the status scale, it is viewed as a hindrance to effective leadership. We must never forget that the model for biblical leadership is servanthood. That has little to do with status and much to do with responsibility. Responsibility does not hinder friendship—but status can.

I believe, however, that the problem is more basic. We live in an age when people do not successfully integrate holiness and love. This is causing havoc in the theology and practice of Christians in almost every area of life. This affects leadership. Just as God's nature is characterized by perfect mingling of holiness and love, leaders also must exemplify this dual nature.

We respond to God's holiness with respect. We "worship God acceptably with reverence and awe, for our 'God is a consuming fire' " (Heb. 12:28-29). We respond to God's love with intimacy. So "we have confidence [or boldness] to enter the Most Holy Place" (Heb. 10:19). In the same way the relationship between a leader and those led is characterized by respect and intimacy.

But today we find it difficult to integrate holiness with love. In the East many fathers are respected by their children but are aloof from them. In the West there is freedom in many families between father and child. But respect is woefully lacking. The same problem affects our relationship with God. Is it any surprise then that people have difficulty when it comes to applying the integrated approach to leadership?

How can leaders who are intimate with those they lead win their respect? By integrating holiness with love. I do not need to describe how the love segment of this relationship is manifested. But some explanation of the holiness of the leader is in order.

The first requirement for a leader's holiness is an exemplary life. Paul told the young Timothy, who was having trouble winning the respect of the members of the church in Ephesus, "Don't let anyone look down on you because you are young, but set an example for the believers in speech, in life, in love, in faith and in purity" (1 Tim. 4:12). This is a more exacting task than enforcing respect through an organizational chart! But it goes to the heart of Christian leadership—which is to lead people into the will of God for the individual and for the organization. And a basic requirement for such leadership is godliness. So Paul urges Timothy to "train [himself] in godliness" (1 Tim. 4:7, RSV).

Just before asking him to be an example, Paul tells Timothy, "Command and teach these things" (1 Tim. 4:11). These are two other things which build respect. To "command" is to give clear instructions. Leaders should know where they are going. Out of their contact with God's word and the issues people face, they should be able to guide people through challenges.

If leaders don't know how to respond to a crisis, they must like Moses seek the face of God and grapple with the issue until they have some idea of what to do. Of course, this grappling must be done in community. But the leader must be involved, without handing the job over to an expert—as many leaders do today (though we do not mean to reject appropriate consulting with experts).

Then the leader must teach, says Paul. This is the supreme ministry activity of Christian leaders. They can't leave the job of teaching to an expert, for biblical leaders lead by teaching. They teach people the truth and ask them to obey the truth. The only ministry-related qualification required of an elder in 1 Timothy 3 is ability to teach. All other qualifications relate to the character of the person.

How far our ideas of leadership seem to be from Paul's! Our leaders are now essentially administrators who leave teaching to others. They have no forum for spiritual-respect-building activities. Then naturally they are also reluctant to participate in intimacy-building activities.

Leaders, because of their holiness, must "correct" and "rebuke" (2 Tim. 4:2). Their intimacy does not prevent their responding to error and sin with indignation. The ability to encourage and to rebuke is essential for integrating love and holiness. These two ministries are placed together by Paul in 2 Timothy 4:2. The leaders hatred of wrong will build respect if backed by exemplary living and loving concern for wrongdoers.

Through the factors mentioned above, respect will be won almost automatically. If leaders are not good examples, if they do not give direction, if they do not teach or rebuke, there will be no biblical foundation for building respect. Such leaders will have to depend on status and rank to get respect. They will find it difficult to develop friendships with those under them.

There is one aspect of freedom and friendship common today, however, which cannot mingle with holiness or respect. This aspect too comes from the failure to integrate holiness with love. I refer to the off-color jokes and unedifying conversations often seen when people let their hair down. Even Christians find it hard to joke without transgressing purity. If leaders participate in such activities with those they lead, they deservedly lose respect.

So today's leaders don't socialize with those led. Instead they socialize with peers and act often in shameful ways at parties and other gatherings with peers. If that is the understanding of socializing people have, then the advice to leaders not to socialize with those under them is understandable.

But that is not the way Christian leaders socialize. They are always holy. And holiness wins the respect of all. If mingled with true concern, holiness will win affection and result in a marked influence for good in the lives of all who follow such leaders.

# THREE

# Friendships in a Fallen World

**W**hile Proverbs has a lot to say about friendship, it does not paint a completely rosy picture about experiences associated with friendship. Proverbs is aware that we live in a fallen world tainted everywhere by sin. Proverbs does not ignore the fact that we must be careful about whom we trust and not be surprised when friendships cause pain and disappointment.

Proverbs 17:17, for example, says lofty things about friends loving at all times and helping in times of trouble. But the next verse warns against trusting people who are not trustworthy. One of the great things about the wisdom of Scripture is its realism. The Bible presents a life of sacrificial love. But not of foolish love.

This is why the Bible is such a trustworthy guide for faith and practice. It is not only an inspiring and comforting devotional book. It is also instructive and practical. Our otherworldly approach to Christian principles often makes Christianity impracticable in day-to-day life. Persons who have an inspiring devotional life which, they say, gives them strength to face the challenges of the day, may be unchristian in their business dealings. They are "inspired' by the Scriptures but not instructed. Biblical wisdom is practical. It has much to say about our day-to-day life in a fallen world.

Wise and prudent persons who want to know how to live in this world would do well to use the Scriptures as their book of instructions for living all of life. This includes family life, business life, social life, religious life, vocational life, and all other areas of life.

### Wisdom About Whom to Trust

Proverbs 17:18 warns, "A man lacking in judgment strikes hands in pledge and puts up security for his neighbor." Proverbs 22:26-27 gives similar advice. "Do not be a man who strikes hands in pledge or puts up security for debts; if you lack the means to pay, your very bed will be snatched from under you."

Striking hands in a pledge refers to shaking hands to seal a business matter. This idea of a covenant (as we saw in chapter one) was what was originally conveyed by shaking hands. So we are told not to go into business deals with those we cannot trust. How many people have gone into business deals, blinded to their dangers by the prospect of quick returns, then faced huge losses!

The second thing to avoid is being guarantor for

someone you don't know well enough to trust fully. It is good to help people in need. But it is foolish to trust strangers. When you act as a guarantor, you say you know someone well enough to be certain the person will keep all commitments. If you cannot be sure of that, then you must not stand up on that person's behalf.

We must quickly add that the above passages are no excuse for not helping people in need. They warn us about the folly of trusting people we don't know. Elsewhere the Bible urges us to give freely to the poor. Proverbs 19:17 says, "He who is kind to the poor lends to the Lord." Jesus said, "Give to the one who asks you, and do not turn away from the one who wants to borrow from you" (Matt. 5:42). Jesus went to the extent of urging us to lend to those who may not pay us back. "And if you lend to those from whom you expect repayment, what credit is that to you? Even 'sinners' lend to 'sinners,' expecting to be repaid in full" (Luke 6:34).

Proverbs 6:1-5 speaks with great urgency about what we should do if people we guarantee fail to fulfill their obligations. Verses 1 and 2 describe the situation the person has gotten into: "My son, if you have put up security for your neighbor, if you have struck hands in a pledge for another, if you have been trapped by what you said, ensnared by the words of your mouth. . . ." Verse 3 tells us what to do in such a situation: "Then do this, my son, to free yourself, since you have fallen into your neighbors hands: Go and humble yourself; press your plea with your neighbor!" Releasing ourselves from these obligations may be humiliating to us as we go and plead with the creditor to release us from them. But that is a price worth paying for our folly.

Verses 4 and 5 stress the urgency of releasing ourselves from these financial obligations. "Allow no sleep to your eyes, no slumber to your eyelids. Free yourself like a gazelle from the hand of the hunter, like a bird from the snare of the fowler." Robert Alden explains the urgency thus: "Don't let another day pass, don't wait until after the siesta. Set the record straight now and get out from under its obligation."

How many Christians today live under the burden of unsettled financial dealings. Such Christians are not free in relationships because they often hide their poor financial management from acquaintances. Mismanagement becomes a big burden for these people, taking away peace and replacing it with anxiety. Unsettled financial matters hinder a Christian's testimony and effectiveness.

Yet it is a mystery to see that an urgency to free themselves from these obligations is not found in the lives of many Christians. They live as if nothing has happened. They spend money on pleasures not essential for survival. While they remain in debt, they say, "I *must* have this," and "I *must* have that."

But these things they "must" have are not crucial for a happy and healthy life. Poor money managers take a vacation at an expensive resort, or go to an expensive restaurant, or buy an expensive dress. When we say we must have these nonessentials at the cost of settling our financial burdens, we show how far we are from the attitude of Christ. He did not even have a place to lay his head when he was on earth!

Willingness to sacrifice freedom from crippling financial obligations for the passing pleasures of materialism is a dangerous trend. Even nations continue affluent lifestyles while their national debt becomes bigger and bigger.

The Bible advocates a life free from the burdens of unsettled financial obligations. It advocates urgency in settling these, because it views the resulting freedom as a great treasure. The very important principle of "short accounts" applies to many spheres of the Christian life and here as well. When we sin we should go to God at once, without delaying the confession. When we hurt someone, we should apologize at once. Similarly when we have financial obligations, we should deal with them at once. Yet many duped by Satan postpone settling accounts and give priority to passing pleasure. Satan wins a great victory when God's children are crippled in this way and rendered ineffective.

## Sensitivity to Each Others' Schedules

Proverbs 25:17 says, "Seldom set foot on your neighbor's house—too much of you, and he will hate you." Kenneth Aitken's title for this verse is "Don't make a pest of yourself." Proverbs says much about the price of friendship. But there is always a good reason for the way we sacrifice for others. Never do we sacrifice for the sake of sacrifice. The price of friendship is always caused by a good purpose. Those who make pests of themselves do not have a good reason for imposing on others.

When we have a genuine need, we may go to a busy friend and get him to give some precious time to help us. We should not be reluctant to do this. This is a necessary feature of commitment. If we say we should not disturb our busy friend in our time of need, we insinuate that our friend is not too committed to us. Our reluctance to go to him is a statement about how we rate our friendship. But some people stay too long in another's presence without good reason. These are selfish people.

Sometimes when my wife is having her devotions, I feel like saying something to her. Often this is a thing that can wait until she has finished her appointment with her Lord. Sometimes I speak without waiting for her devotions to be over. Then I act in the way this passage condemns. I unnecessarily impose on her.

The key to this verse is sensitivity and consideration. Friends should be sensitive to the situations other people face. If my mother-in-law is at our home and is talking to my wife when I come home from work, she leaves the room. This is not because she does not like me, but because this a time I want to be with my wife. My mother-in-law's concern for us makes her leave the room.

## Sinful Sexual Relationships

Adultery is a sinful form of friendship; Proverbs has much to say about its lure and dangers. There are vivid warnings to keep away from situations that could open us to temptation. Proverbs 5:3-5 says, "For the lips of an adulteress [or adulterer!] drip honey, and her speech is smoother than oil; but in the end she is bitter as gall, sharp as a double-edged sword. Her feet go down to death; her steps lead straight to the grave." At first adulterous relationships are greatly attractive. But they drag us down to the way of death.

A vivid description of how a person falls into sexual temptation is given in Proverbs 7. The young person had probably not planned to fall into temptation. He was seduced. That was possible because he was "a youth who lacked judgment" (7:7). One evening, as he was walking down the street, "out came a woman to meet him, dressed like a prostitute and with crafty intent" (7:10). (It should be remembered, of course, that the seducer could as easily be a man.) Verses 13-20 describe how "with persuasive words she led him astray; she seduced him with her smooth talk" (7:21).

There was a powerful attraction to what she offered. She said, "Come, let's drink deep of love till morning; let's enjoy ourselves with love!" (7:18). The immediate satisfaction and thrill that comes from sexual sin gives it great appeal. This appeal is intensified in today's society where the motto "If it feels good, then it's got to be right" is so popular. In such an environment, men or women faced with temptation find it difficult to resist.

The young man seems to have been undecided how to respond to this seduction. But suddenly passion rules him and good sense ceases to influence him. "All at once he followed her like an ox going to the slaughter, like a deer stepping into a noose" (7:22). How many have been carried away by passion, doing things they would not do if in their proper senses. But the young man was in the wrong place. He had "entertained" the temptation for too long. Now he was powerless to resist.

This episode brings out the wisdom of Paul's advice to Timothy. "Flee the evil desires of youth" (2 Tim. 2:22). We must not negotiate with sin. In certain situations it is best to leave the scene of temptation immediately, as Joseph did when seduced by Potiphar's wife while he was alone in the house with her (Gen. 39:12).

The section ends with a warning: "Now then, my sons, listen to me; pay attention to what I say. Do not let your heart turn to her ways or stray into her paths. Many are the victims she has brought down" (Prov. 7:24-26a). This type of warning is found over and over in Proverbs (1:10-11; 2:16-19; 5:1-23; 6:20-35; 9:13-18; 22:14; 23:26-28; 30:18-20).

The frequency of these warnings should sober us. The point is that, because sexual passions can be easily aroused and difficult to control, wise people are doubly careful in this area. Proverbs 30:18-20 says, "There are three things that are too amazing for me, four that I do not understand: the way of an eagle in the sky, the way of a snake on a rock, the way of a ship on the high seas, and the way of a man with a maiden." This type of care is a key feature of the wisdom which Proverbs 2:16 says "will save you also from the adulteress [or adulterer]."

The heart of wisdom, however, is having the Word of God always close. Proverbs 7:1-4 describes this.

> My son, keep my words and store up my commands within you. Keep my commands and you will live; guard my teachings as the apple of your eye. Bind them on your fingers; write them on the tablet of your heart.

These verses describe an intimate contact with and careful attitude toward the Word. It is interesting that these four verses about our attitude toward the Word are the prologue to the chapter we looked at about the seductress and the young man who lacked judgment. The idea is that one who conscientiously seeks to know and obey the will of God will be sensitive to the approach of temptation. This attitude is well described in a hymn by Charles Wesley, "I Want a Principle Within" (1749).

I want a principle within
of watchful, godly fear,
a sensibility of sin,
a pain to feel it near.

I want the first approach to feel
of pride or wrong desire,
to catch the wandering of my will,
and quench the kindling fire.

From thee that I may no more may stray,
no more thy goodness grieve,
grant me the filial awe, I pray,
the tender conscience give.

Quick as the apple of an eye,
O God, my conscience make;
awake my soul when sin is nigh,
and keep it still awake.

## The Vulnerability of Friendship

The word *'allup* is the strongest possible label to use for friendship. It carries the idea of bosom companion. But it is used three times to describe the vulnerability of friendship. The first time is in Proverbs 2:16-17 which speaks of 'the wayward wife . . . who has left the partner (*'allup*) of her youth and ignored the covenant she made before God." Here we are presented the pain of a marriage broken through the unfaithfulness of a partner.

The other two times the word *'allup* appears in connection with the vulnerability of friendship are in descriptions of the way loose talk can destroy friendship. Proverbs 16:28 says, "A gossip separates close friends." Proverbs 17:9 says, "Whoever repeats the matter [of an offense committed by a friend] separates close friends." These sobering proverbs remind us that there are limitations to what we can expect from friendships. They can fail us. And when that happens, we end up deeply hurt.

Now because of this some people never cultivate close friendships. But that is not biblical. Remember that even Jesus had to face the pain of having his disciple Judas betray him. But he placed a high priority on his relationship with his close friends, the disciples. This ought to comfort us and challenge our reluctance to cultivate close friendships.

## The Primacy of Friendship with God

More important, the references to the vulnerability of friendship teach us that all human friendships are limited in their scope and reliability. Always our most important relationship must be with God. Those who jeopardize their relationship with God are sacrificing the eternal for the temporal. Even our spouses must never take a higher place than God.

Of course, this is in keeping with the teaching of Proverbs. Before launching into all the great words of wisdom, Proverbs first gives us the basis for all this wisdom. Proverbs 1:7 says, "The fear of the Lord is the beginning of knowledge." We must never read Proverbs without this perspective. It is a book of wisdom.

Some of the wisdom found in Proverbs is found in other religions also. But what makes Proverbs unique is that for children of God all wisdom springs from our relationship with God. Proverbs 3:5-6 teaches the primacy of our relationship with God even more vividly. "Trust in the Lord with all your heart and lean not on your own understanding; in all your ways acknowledge him and he will make your paths straight." So our relationship with God is what is basic.

But putting God first does not hurt human friendships. It only strengthens them. This is what gives the foundation for a stable friendship. You see, if our stability comes from God and we expect total goodness from God alone, we will be secure people. Those whose security is in God will not try to grab security from other people. Insecure people who look to other humans for their primary source of security put a huge burden on these other people. Such persons expect so much from friends or spouses that their relationships become big burdens on others. Because the other persons are afraid not to perform according to expectations, they are not free to enjoy such relationships.

It is right to have expectations of people, but these must not be unrealistic. The trouble is that insecure people try to grab from fallible people things they can get from God alone—such as absolute perfection and personal security.

Those who find their security in God can risk loving others. The love may be rejected, or the loved one may fail and disappointment may result. But the Christian has the strength to go on because the earthly relationship is not the most important thing in life. Some people don't want to risk loving because they are afraid that it might result in disappointment. As Christians, we know that even if we are disappointed the most important thing in life, our relationship with God, is not touched. Nothing can separate us from the love of Christ. So we can handle the battering that comes from the disappointments of earthly love.

But there is more to our relationship with God than security. The glory of the gospel is that our relationship with God is not some supra-spiritual reality disconnected from the hard realities of life in a hostile and fallen world. We go to God through Jesus Christ. And Jesus is our brother and friend. Hebrews 2:17 puts this strikingly: "For this reason he had him to be made like his brothers in every way, in order that he might become a merciful and faithful high priest in service to God." By becoming our brother, Jesus could be our high priest, that is, our mediator.

The writer of Hebrews makes a further point about the brotherhood of Jesus in the next verse. "Because he himself suffered when he was tempted, he is able to help those who are being tempted." Jesus suffered when he was tempted! He did not sail through temptation with consummate ease as we would have expected the Son of God to do. But that suffering qualified him to be our brother, to identify with us.

When we go to God with our struggles, he does not simply look at us with condescending benevolence and drop some sufficient grace from heaven. Rather, because God knows our pain, he not only gives us strength to face it, he comes up to us as a comforting friend.

And how much we need a friend in times of trouble. It is such a source of release to be able to say, "At least he understands." When we weep, it is a comfort to know that Jesus also wept. When we are betrayed by our friends, it is a comfort to know that Jesus also was betrayed. When people in whom we have placed trust fail us, it is a comfort to know that, after three years of constant companionship and training, Peter denied Christ.

So if you are going into close friendships, be prepared to be hurt. Don't count on what you should expect from God alone. If you do, your hurt will damage you permanently. If your trust is in God, you will still be hurt, because God made you with the capacity to love. That capacity includes in it vulnerability to personal hurt. But the hurt will drive you to God—to bask in his comfort, to lean on his love. In fact, the hurt will drive you closer to God. Your bitterness will wash away along with the tears that you shed in God's presence.

You may continue to be sad, because the earthly conditions may not change. But you will not be broken or bitter. The most important thing about your life is still intact. You are loved of God. So amidst the pain there is a brightness in you that love alone can give.

Let me speak directly to you. Have you been deeply hurt? A lover has disappointed you. A marriage that started with much promise has turned sour. A person you invested much in has betrayed you. Go to Jesus! He knew what it was to be betrayed by his close friend. But he will never betray you. Lean on his gentle breast. And weep away your bitterness as you release your burdens upon him.

Jesus will not only heal you; he will also draw you nearer to himself than you were before. Later, when you look back at the pain, there may still be sorrow. But there will not be bitterness. Bitterness by now has been replaced by the love of God in your heart. So you will be grateful to God—grateful for the way he healed you, grateful for the things he taught you through these experiences.

# FOUR

# *Unselfish Commitment*

**W**e are talking in this book of friends who stick closer to us than a sibling (Prov. 18:24). The word translated here as "sticks" is the same word used of Ruth clinging to her mother-in-law, Naomi (Ruth 1:14). Commitment is the basic idea. In this and the chapters that follow we will see how Proverbs and Ecclesiastes describe a commitment that sticks.

## *Selfish Relationships*

Commitment is out of fashion today. Many of our relationships are selfish. Proverbs speaks often about selfish relationships. Proverbs 14:20 says, "The poor are shunned even by their neighbors, but the rich have many friends." Proverbs 19:4 says something very similar: "Wealth brings many friends, but a poor man's friend deserts him." Both verses condemn the insincerity of people who befriend the rich because of what they can get from them and neglect the poor because they are of no use to them (or so they think).

This type of behavior is not alien to us today. Just look at the way a church usher welcomes a rich and influential person at the entrance to a church. Then compare the treatment the usher gives a badly dressed and desperately poor person. That may reveal to us how utilitarian we are in our approach to people. Actually, rarely do such poor people enter our churches. They feel so uncomfortable and unwelcome in an average church that they usually don't like to come in to the churches. (This gives us a strong reason to dress simply when we go to church. But that is another topic!)

Proverbs 19:6 says, "Many curry favor with a ruler, and everyone is the friend of a man who gives gifts." For a modern expression of this, we can go to an international Christian conference. We will see that people often ignore the unknown delegates in favor of the famous people. Some go to the extent of bringing gifts for these famous people—the very persons who may least need gifts. While talking to an "unknown saint," persons may break off the conversation in the middle of a sentence and start talking to a famous Christian who has just appeared.

The rich, the generous, and the powerful may have many friends. We may even be tempted to envy the powerful because of this. But that is because we are so blinded by the lure of immediate, shallow satisfaction that prominence can bring. Actually, we should feel sorry for powerful people who have this type of friend.

For it is so hard for them to find real friends. And if they fall from their positions of power, as is so common, their friends desert them.

How unlike the Christian model all this is. It is, of course, the marketing model of many businesses, which set apart large sums of money to curry favor with influential people. But the Bible presents God and his followers as eager to befriend and help needy people. In fact, a key way to test people's Christian character is to observe the way they treat insignificant people when they think no one is watching.

The principle we glean from this is that many friendships are essentially selfish. Our commitment has actually been to what the person can do for us, not to the person. We want that person's wealth or power. Or we want the work that the person does for the group that he or she belongs to. When the person wants to leave the group, we forget all our earlier concern. The friendship remains only as long as it helps us. This is an age of disposable relationships.

Daniel Yankelovich, respected analyst of North American social trends and public attitudes, has written *New Rules: Searching for Self-fulfillment in a World Turned Upside Down*. In his book, Yankelovich shows that in Western society, where the aim of people is self-fulfillment, a new set of rules has developed. Such rules are beginning to appear in developing nations as well. One of these new rules is that lasting commitments are out. We remain committed to an organization or person so long as we think it benefits us. We drop any commitment which ceases to help us.

## Leaving a Group

There may come a time when persons must leave a group they have been committed to. Perhaps there is no suitable place in the organization for persons with their abilities. Perhaps their vision can best be fulfilled elsewhere. Perhaps they are moving to a new area and need to find a new church. At such times, the Christian model is to make the transition as helpful as possible to those who are leaving.

Yet people are often hurt by the way groups they worked with drop them when the group feels it has no place for them. They labored so sacrificially. Now the group just drops them! Leaders of such groups are certainly not friends who stick closer than brothers or sisters.

When a daughter decides it is time to leave home, her parents don't drop their concern for her. They do everything to make the transition as smooth as possible. Just as parents help a daughter, so should leaders of groups aid those who are leaving the group.

The leaders might, for example, use contacts they may have to help find good jobs for persons leaving their organization. When church members leave an area, churches can do their best to commend departing members to a new congregation, thus aiding such people's smooth transition into a new community.

If persons leave an organization to pursue further studies, leaders can try to raise some funds for such studies. Usually we fund only studies of those who will work for us after the studies are over. But how about those who have served us faithfully and sacrificially for many years and now sense it is time to leave us? Is all we give them the gratuity government laws require? No. Our righteousness must exceed that of the scribes and Pharisees. We may be called to help fund their education because of our gratitude and concern for them.

If we adopt a generous attitude, departure of workers from a group can honor the Lord. Persons can leave feeling loved by co-workers. They do not have to apply for jobs in secret, then suddenly announce their departure—to the consternation of all. The young believers are often the ones most hurt. What has happened to all the teaching they received about fellowship, when persons who taught these things contradict all they taught and suddenly leave?

Sometimes we may ask persons to leave a group for disciplinary reasons. That does not, however, eliminate our responsibility to show concern. We may, for example, help persons forced to leave paid Christian service to find jobs in the business world.

It may at first seem costly for a group to be committed to people as described above. But such groups will be blessed with committed members. Commitment breeds commitment. And what a great blessing committed people are in an age where commitment has gone out of fashion.

## Covenant Love and Discipline

It is significant that the great word *hesed*, used in the Old Testament to describe God's covenant-keeping love for Israel, appears in Proverbs to describe friendship. 19:22 says, "What a man desires is unfailing love; better to be poor than a liar." The NIV translates *hesed* as "unfailing love." Aitken and the RSV translate it as "loyalty." The idea is that just as God remains faithful to his covenant with Israel whatever the situation, we must be faithful to our friends.

In the following chapters, we will see ways this loyalty manifests itself. Here we will look at one aspect of covenant-keeping loyalty usually not associated with contemporary understandings of loyalty.

The Old Testament covenants included stipulations. And in covenant-making rituals, blessings for keeping the covenant and curses for breaking it were often read. Old Testament history shows that God's loyalty to Israel did not condone sin. When Israel sinned God judged. But he did not give up on the Israelites.

Similarly when a friend sins, we don't ignore the sin. We back whatever just discipline is meted out to the person. Proverbs 15:10 speaks of this type of disciplining: "Stern discipline awaits him who leaves the path."

Church discipline is another biblical practice rarely seen in the church. I suppose that is to be expected in churches that seem to be dedicated to making people feel good. Disciplining does not feel good. It feels bad—not only to persons disciplining, but also to those disciplined and to the other members of the church.

Indeed, the work of disciplining wrongdoers is one of the most unpleasant aspects of a leader's work. Often something in a leader says, "Ignore the problem." Sometimes other Christians take this ignoring as a sign of patience. This is why we hear people say, "He's such a saint. He will never scold someone."

Such "patience" is not saintliness but an expression of our fallenness. Not disciplining happens when we don't take sin as seriously as God does. We often prefer to have the nice feeling that comes from being accommodating of everybody. So we ignore sin when we should be confronting it.

People who ignore discipline often seem nice. But, as someone has said, "Nice guys have no cutting edge." No one dislikes them. But they cannot significantly influence sinners to walk the path of holiness.

Christians often take one of three inadequate routes when confronted by the need to discipline. First, they avoid disciplining a useful person because the cost is considered too much. Say a talented musician commits a serious indiscretion. This becomes known shortly before an important musical program. If biblical discipline were carried out, he would not appear in public. But without him the program would be greatly hampered.

So the musician appears on the program. But this violates the covenant relationship we have with him. Christian love includes commitment to respond to wrongdoing with justice.

The second inadequate approach is to attack the problem too late. There is no regular opportunity for advising and rebuking the person because her supervisor is too distant from her. Sometimes the supervisor does not even know what is happening. Other times the supervisor is reluctant to advise and rebuke because it simply does not seem appropriate with a person one is not too close to.

But sometimes the problem grows serious. At that stage a disciplinary inquiry must be conducted, resulting in widespread heartache. Often what could have been dealt with earlier with a few words of advice or rebuke has unnecessarily become a major crisis.

The third inadequate approach is to discipline persons, then forget about them because they cannot help anymore in our program. That too is unloving, for our commitment is not primarily to persons' talents. Though we may not use them in our programs, we can meet with and spend time trying to restore them at this time when they so need companionship.

The only time we are justified in rejecting a person is after all approaches have been tried and the person concerned rejects all overtures. Such a person's heart has been hardened. We should refuse to accept anyone into fellowship whose heart is hard.

In 1 John 1:7 we read that to have fellowship with one another we must first walk in the light. This does not mean people must be perfect. This verse next talks of being cleansed from sin. Christians who have sinned badly can have fellowship with other Christians. In fact, they really need fellowship after they have fallen. But if the fellowship is going to be deep, they must first accept their sinfulness—that is, confess their sin. Then they can walk in the light.

If they chose not to do this, we cannot ignore the refusal. We may be called on to refuse association with such sinners in the hope that the pain of our rejection will provide a redemptive jolt. Jesus said that after all has been tried and they still refuse to repent, we must treat them as we would a pagan or a tax collector (Matt. 18:15-17). R. T. France comments on this passage that "after all persuasion has failed, a cold shoulder may still bring him to his senses"(p. 275). Paul handed over Hymenaeus and Alexander to Satan, that is, expelled them from the fellowship, so that they might be "taught not to blaspheme" (1 Tim. 1:20).

This is the price of Christian friendship. It is easier to ignore the sin and continue the friendship. But if we do this, we are unfaithful to the sinners. And we act differently than God does with his covenant people.

## *Commitment to Pray*

There is an aspect of commitment to one another which, to my knowledge, does not appear in Proverbs but is found often in the Old and New Testaments. This is the commitment to pray for one another. While we have a general commitment to pray for a large number of people, we have a special commitment to pray for those particularly close to us. Paul told his special friend and spiritual child that "night and day I constantly remember you in my prayers" (2 Tim. 1:3).

Prayer is like fuel to a Christian relationship. The most important tie in Christian friendship is our common union with Christ. Therefore, it is essentially a spiritual fellowship. So when we talk to God about another person, we are strengthening our tie with that person.

We can pray even at great distance from one another. Prayer helps me remain close to my family and colleagues as I travel. On my trips I cannot spend time talking with them, but I can pray for them daily. And I know they pray for me. This prayer for one another maintains spiritual closeness.

There is a word here for leaders. We have special

ties of friendship with those we supervise. As their leaders we are their servants. The greatest service we can do for them is to pray for them as Paul did for Timothy. It is significant that the only mention in the Gospels of Jesus talking about his own prayer life is when he told Peter that he had prayed for him (Luke 22:32).

During the time Vedanayakam Azariah was Bishop of the Anglican Church in South India, the church experienced a great revival and many Hindus were added to it. It has been said that one of the secrets of his effectiveness as bishop was his practice of praying daily for each pastor in his diocese.

The apostles in the early church asked that they be separated for prayer and the ministry of the word (Acts 6:4). One aspect of the prayer mentioned here must have been praying for those they led. Like Moses did so many times, we are called to intercede on behalf of those we lead. Prayer should be a basic feature in the job description of a Christian leader. The prophet Samuel regarded as a sin the failure to pray for the people whose spiritual leader he was. He told Israel, "As for me, far be it from me that I should sin against the Lord by failing to pray for you" (1 Sam. 12:23).

Not only do we pray for others, we ask others to pray for us. Thus we affirm our ties with others. In eight of his thirteen letters, Paul asks readers to pray for him. In ten of Paul's letters, he mentions praying for his readers.

This suggests it is good to tell our friends we pray for them. That news will certainly encourage persons for whom we pray, especially when they are going through difficult times. It will also deepen ties between those praying and those prayed for.

# Commitment in Times of Trouble

**W**e have said that commitment is the key to Christian friendships. But commitment is also a word which has suffered from that inflation of meaning in which words are cheapened and lose their original significance. The fact that a person claims to be committed to another does not necessarily mean the commitment is genuine. It is when a person is in trouble that we can really know whether the commitment of a friend is real.

### The Unfaithful
Proverbs 25:19 says, "Like a bad tooth or a lame foot is reliance on the unfaithful in times of trouble." People depend on their teeth and feet for eating and walking, which are basic functions of life. A bad tooth or lame foot are important parts which have failed the body.

The proverb is saying that we may depend on someone for help in crisis and find that the person has failed us. The importance of commitment also emerges in this verse. We see this in the word *unfaithful*. A true friend is faithful.

A sad instance of unfaithfulness is described in 2 Timothy 4:16, where Paul says, "At my first defense, no one came to my support, but everyone deserted me." One of history's greatest warriors was on trial for the gospel, and Christians did not want to associate with him. It simply was not personally advantageous (according to earthly values) to be committed to Paul at that time.

Why do we forsake people who are in trouble? Because it costs to love at such times. Sometimes the cost we seek to avoid is *the shame of associating with people who are down*. This is what Paul had to face when he went to his trial.

We see such unfaithfulness today in the workplace. The division head has suddenly started finding fault all the time with your friend who has long been a faithful hard worker. But to cut costs management has decided to discontinue his services and is looking for ways to highlight his shortcomings. You see what is happening and realize you have no guarantee your own place in the company is secure. You want to be in management's good graces. So when the boss speaks ill of your friend, you agree, not because the boss is right, but because you don't want to jeopardize your place in the company.

Such behavior is so common that people accept it as normal. Many have come to believe that selfishness of this sort is a necessary evil in a competitive society. Yet Scripture condemns such unfaithfulness. We too must abstain from and condemn lack of faithfulness. We need to help people realize it is a dirty thing to forsake a friend for their own convenience.

Failing to help a friend is a sin of omission and, therefore, may be overlooked. Such failure rarely appears in a catalogue of common sins. But it is a common sin, thus we must address it.

A common reason given for not helping others in need is that *there is no time for it.* Here the cost is the inconvenience of giving time to help a person in need. We may need to visit the person and spend time with her when she is depressed or facing a crisis. We may need to do some things for her if she is confined to a bed or overloaded with too much to do.

When a friend has a crisis, then it becomes an urgent problem for us. However busy we are, we do something to help her. Usually the really busy people are the only ones who will have time.

I once saw a sign that said, "If you want something done, ask the busy people. They are the only ones who will have the time." Such people somehow find the time to help. They have a lasting influence for good in this world. They invest at personal cost in the lives of others and change people through their ministry and example.

There are many nice people in the world who never have such influence. Few speak ill of them. They have not harmed anyone. But the people they help are generally limited to their own family circle. They will not inconvenience themselves to get involved in the problems of others. They may be nice people, but they dishonor Christ, who told his followers, "As the Father has sent me, I am sending you" (John 20:21).

Christ's model of sacrificial service is now our model. We are people who give our lives for our friends like Christ did (John 15:12-13). To fail to do this is to dishonor Christ.

Indeed, it is often true that we don't have time to help people in need. But loving, busy people *make* time, despite the cost. We somehow find time for our priorities. For Christians, the needs of friends are a priority. So we will make the time.

I realize this lifestyle is not popular today. That is partly because some Christians have done Christian service irresponsibly. They have neglected their families. They have ruined their health. They have done things others could have done—all in the name of service.

But there is responsible costly service. This is the balanced-life approach. Living the balanced life does not mean doing everything in moderation, though this is what it means to many. Moderation is often an excuse for taking things easy. The Christian living a balanced life is obedient in every area of life. So one who helps others is committed to finding time for family also.

Balanced living can be hard. After an exhausting time of counseling a troubled friend, you may not feel like talking in depth to your spouse, even if you should. You may feel like going to bed or watching television. Obedient Christians will make themselves talk to their spouses, even though they do not feel like it, because that is their Christian responsibility.

I must add that if you obey in this way, God will give you the strength and sustain you. This is the miracle of God's faithfulness to the obedient. Paul says, "I labor, struggling with all his energy, which so powerfully works in me" (Col. 1:29). There is labor and struggle, but there is also God's energy which works powerfully in us. God's energy makes life exciting and meaningful. Those who play it safe by living for themselves will never know the excitement of having the power of God work through them.

I believe that the cross many of us are called to bear is the balanced life. We often see persons so involved in ministry that they neglect their family life. Or those so dedicated to family they neglect their responsibility to be active in ministry. Both styles are easy ways out. The difficult path is trying to do both. This is the way of balance, the way of the cross.

The same principle applies to the need for rest. If you lose sleep because you helped a person in need, then you are responsible to use your creativity to get sleep another time. People point out that you can never recover lost sleep. True, but there is a price to pay for a life of service. Here we labor and toil (Col. 1:29). We have a whole eternity to rest from our labors (Rev. 14:13).

Of course, when you hear that someone is in trouble that does not mean you are the only person who can help. The leader who gets too much ego gratification from ministry falls into that trap. Such people can drive themselves to complete exhaustion by making their ministries too dependent on themselves. Sometimes when we hear that someone needs help, our task may be simply to ensure the person receives aid. We are motivated by concern for that person's welfare and will be happy if the person is helped, even though we may not do the helping.

We must not let abuses of the principle of sacrificial service deter us from involvement in it. Our age has many slogans about friendship. Shops carry different kinds of cards on friendship that can be mailed to our friends. We frequently hear people say, "I love you." In some circles hugging as a sign of friendship has become popular. But all these things have grown cheap; they are not accompanied by costly commitment.

## *For Better, for Worse*

Proverbs 17:17 also presents the idea of the faithfulness of friendship being evidenced when there is trouble. It says, "A friend loves at all times, and a brother is born for adversity." "A friend loves at all times" is another way of saying "for better, for worse; for richer, for poorer; in sickness and in health; till death do us part." Christian friendships are not fair-weather relationships. This principle applies absolutely to marriage but also has a bearing on other friendships.

Let us apply the principle of loyal friendship to the marriage relationship—that key friendship. Marriage has been under fire in the West. One response has been to highlight the romance of marriage. There are many books on how to bring the spark back into marriage. There is much emphasis on the fact that love is an enjoyable thing, which, of course, is true.

The emphasis on the romance of marriage is good. But romance is useless without commitment, becoming a hollow enjoyment. When troubles come, romance vanishes. When a child or one partner gets sick, there may be no possibility for so-called romantic activities. You can't, for example, go on vacation when someone is seriously ill. At such times relationships always face special strains. But relationships too dependent on romance face even greater strains. Sometimes such relationships become such a burden that they are dropped. I have often wondered whether this has something to do with the number of divorces that take place after a family crisis. For example, I know of parents who divorced after enduring a long struggle because of a child's sickness.

Commitment gives a security on which you can build romance. Christian love does have include romance. But because such love springs from commitment, it is more enjoyable and deeply satisfying than love based only on shallow romance. You don't have doubts at the back of your mind that this may not last. With such doubts you cannot fully love a person or fully enjoy the love relationship. With commitment there is a mixture of security and freedom which makes the romance truly enjoyable.

Does the principle of sticking to relationships still apply when serious incompatibility arises? Incompatibility is a popular word today. I believe that is a symptom of the devotion of this age to self-fulfillment. When self-fulfillment is defined to preclude personal suffering, then incompatibility becomes a grounds for divorce. The divorce epidemic in turn is a symptom of our society's inability to face suffering.

Christian commitment in marriage comes out of the belief that, when the marriage vow to be faithful to the end was made, being faithful to the spouse became God's will. That commitment gives us strength to face up to problems and work on solutions. This is easier if both spouses are Christians. But even then, given our weaknesses, commitment will not be easy. There will be struggle, there will be pain. But the commitment eliminates the option of splitting up. Many couples have found that, after many stormy and painful years, finally God's grace won through and a joyous relationship emerged.

Other couples have not seen such resolution, perhaps because one partner was particularly difficult and inflexible. Then the other partner chose the path of suffering and refused to give up trying for a resolution. He or she had a whole eternity to enjoy the rewards of faithfulness in heaven. But even on earth, we often find that this person was blessed by children grateful for his or her faithfulness.

Such thinking sounds strange today. This is because even many Christians have swallowed the approach to life of putting immediate fulfillment above eternal principles. Biblical Christianity says commitments are worth sticking to even through suffering.

For the Christian suffering is normal. In fact, to enjoy a truly deep relationship with Jesus we *must* suffer. He was a suffering servant, and to be like him we also must suffer. This is why Paul desired the fellowship of sharing in Christ's suffering (Phil. 3:10). There is a depth of oneness with Christ that comes only through suffering. We may have pain difficult to bear. But in the midst of the pain, we know a nearness to Christ that fulfills us. Though in pain, we experience a fullness that leaves us ultimately more complete than the restless pleasure seekers who don't know the meaning of commitment. For the Christian, suffering is purposeful, so we will not compromise our principles to avoid suffering.

The attempt to have pleasure without commitment dooms people to shallow emptiness. They have their entertainment, their vacations, their precious independence. But they are doomed to remain unfulfilled. They have tried to construct an unreal world—a world without pain and suffering. Those who accept suffering as a necessary part of life are not surprised when it comes. They aren't filled with the disillusionment that many have when they experience suffering. This disillusionment is what makes suffering so unbearable to many.

I do not want to increase the guilt and pain you feel if you are divorced. The step has been taken. God can heal and start a new life for you. If you have confessed any sin that may have contributed to the divorce and handed yourself to God for his care and direction, God will surely help you start a new life bright with the possibilities of grace. You will face the pain of loneliness and regret over the past. But God will compensate with his presence and direction, enabling you to experience the full life Christ alone can give (John 10:10).

My desire is to encourage those who are suffering or will face suffering because of commitments they have made. God may be calling them to endure pain and through that show the world that there are deeper springs of fulfillment that can coexist with pain.

Proverbs 17:17 says that "a brother is born for adversity." Derek Kidner explains, "In trouble you see what family ties are, and you also see who are your friends." Again the point is that the best time to test friendship is when there are problems. Actually times of trouble are a good time to test not only friendship but also a person's character.

## Self-Fulfillment Through Friendship

Proverbs 27:10 has something to say about friendship and trouble. "Do not forsake your friend and the friend of your father, and do not go to your brothers house when disaster strikes you—better a neighbor nearby than a brother far away."

The first part of this verse is a plea to keep up our friendships. The second part tells us what to do when we have an urgent need. We won't have time to search for family members who live far away. So it is good to have friends nearby. They will help us when we are in trouble.

This reminds us again that commitment in friendship is not just an obligation we must dutifully perform. Friendship is a help to us. Some seeking self-fulfillment may reject deep commitments because they see them as an unhelpful waste of time and energy. But all the so-called sacrifices of Christianity yield results beneficial to us. Jesus said that those who lose their life for the sake of the gospel will end up finding it. This principle applies to the cost of friendship too.

The irony is that those who give up commitment

for the sake of self-fulfillment do not truly fulfill them-selves. Obedient Christians are the ones who are really self-fulfilled. It is typical of the deception of Satan to lead people away from the truth in search of some-thing only the truth can give them. Thus people who can't be bothered with deep ties with others are lonely and unhappy, especially when in trouble. This is seen particularly when they are old.

Now more than ever, Christians should be reflect-ing on the truth that when we are made captives of the Lord, then truly we are set free. Commitment may seem to restrict us, but it is the only way to freedom.

# SIX

# *Wisdom Through Friends*

**W**e ended the last chapter by stating that friendships offer us many blessings. In this chapter we will look at the blessing of increased wisdom that comes to us through friends.

### *Advice Regarding Our Plans*

Proverbs often mentions the need to seek advice when making plans. Proverbs 15:22 says, "Plans fail for lack of counsel, but with many advisers they succeed." Proverbs 20:18 applies this principle to warfare: "Make plans by seeking advice; if you wage war, obtain guidance" (see also 11:14).

This principle can be applied to many areas of our lives. If you are in some sort of ministry, it may apply to a strategy for ministry you are about to adopt. It could apply to plans you have to expand your work or to add on something to your house. It could also apply to that all-important decision you make regarding your life partner. It could apply to the way you respond to people you have to deal with in some way.

I can think of at least two reasons why we need advice regarding our plans. First, we often have emotional attachments to our own plans which may blind us to the pitfalls. These are our visions, the products of our creative efforts. We are so excited about the strong points that we don't see the weak points. Second, selfishness can influence us to act in ways unbecoming to holy people. We may not realize our actions were motivated by selfishness until someone points it out.

We will begin by looking at an example of how our *emotions* can adversely affect our decisions. A young man is consumed by attraction to a young woman. He believes this is true love. He becomes convinced that this is the person he is going to marry. He talks to the woman about marriage. She accepts his proposal. They announce their engagement. A perceptive friend, not blinded by the emotional force of attraction, sees that some real problems can be expected if these two marry. But at this stage it seems too late to offer advice. After the first glow of marriage fades, the spouses realize how mismatched they are. For the rest of their lives, they regret their decision.

A similar thing can happen when a person chooses a new job. The prospective employer promises the skies and the future employee is blinded by the attractiveness of this job. One able to see the job more objectively may see pitfalls not obvious to the job-seeker.

Why do people who know the value of advice ignore it when making important decisions? Some people have an idea that a truly romantic courtship must not involve down-to-earth conversations with friends about the suitability of this tie. Some regard such recourse to friends as a violation of their independence. With the growth of individualism, this is becoming a more and more common reason for neglecting advice in decision making. Others are so determined to follow their instincts that—blinded by the force of attraction—they do not want to hear a negative word. We must recognize our fallibility and ask for advice from trusted friends.

In recent years we have seen many clergy divorces. Often a main cause for the divorce is that the spouse was not willing to adopt the lifestyle required of a clergy spouse. It soon becomes clear they should never have married. But swept away by love, they ignored their differences and took the plunge. We should not only blame the spouse. The minister was unfair to expect the spouse to adopt a lifestyle he or she was not willing to adopt. They simply were mismatched.

I once asked an American clergyman whether an average ministerial candidate or minister gets any input from the ministerial community about choice of spouse. He said that there was no structure to facilitate such input. I thought this scandalous! What is the use of all this talk of community if the community cannot help its ministers when they make their most important decisions? My clergy friend even went on to say that people prefer not to talk about their personal lives at ministerial meetings because that could jeopardize their progress up the ecclesiastical status ladder.

I must hasten to add that there is hope for a mismatched couple. God can change situations as his grace acts on people and situations and brings healing. There are no irreconcilable differences if we open ourselves to God. The commitment people have to each other and the openness to God's molding can lead to healing. Of course, given our human weaknesses, the path may be long and painful. Alas, as we said in the last chapter, many are not willing to suffer. The price of healing seems too high. The time for healing seems too long.

This then is an area where our emotions can deceive us. Now let us look at the area of personal relationships where *selfishness* can also cause wrong decisions. Some acquaintances affirm our egos. They hang onto our every word. They frequently compliment us, and we are comfortable in their presence. Others don't affirm us in this way. Perhaps they are not attracted to our way of doing things. Their personalities may be such that they do not relate warmly to people. Perhaps they were friendly with our predecessor and are disappointed that she was moved. So they will take time to accept us. The people who do not praise us are not bad. But their reaction to us is a blow to our pride.

We can be inaccurate in our judgments with both these groups of people because we are influenced by the way they affect our egos. I once heard the late Sri Lankan churchman D. T. Niles say that we generally categorize people into two groups. We regard the people we like as good and others as bad. When the "good" people do something wrong, we excuse it. When the "bad" people do something right, we attribute wrong motives to them. We favor the "good" people and are prejudiced against the "bad" people.

Team members will help us avoid these errors in judgment. They will see when our decisions which have been influenced (often subconsciously) by our selfishness are wrong, and help us correct them.

Let me share two specific areas where I have seen errors of the type mentioned above. I have found, often too late, that persons may relate in one way to leaders and in a very different way to peers and subordinates. They may be respectful and kind to their leaders but treat peers and subordinates with disdain.

I have also found, again often too late, that we are sometimes inaccurate in judgments about people we disciple. These are people we regard as our spiritual children. We tend to overlook their weaknesses and too readily accept their explanations of errors. Because of our ambitions for them, we like to see them progress. So we may promote them to positions for which they are unsuited. Like most parents, we are not very objective about the abilities of our "children."

This is why, when making decisions related to discipline or promotions, it is important to get the advice of others who will be frank. Team members can help us be more accurate in judgments about such people.

### Advice Regarding Our Behavior

Proverbs 12:15 says, "The way of a fool seems right to him, but a wise man listens to advice." The thrust of this verse is that we must not be too confident about the rightness of our motives and actions. Our friends see things we may not see. Here are two examples.

Christians often get emotionally entangled with members of the opposite sex without realizing what is happening. The trouble may happen with a person with whom you work closely, with someone you give a daily ride to work, or with a person you are counseling. You feel good about being able to help this person. But through the prolonged contact an unhealthy emotional tie is developing. You begin to say things you should share only with your spouse.

Yet these relationships are often regarded as "just another Christian friendship." Our minds have a way of deluding us like that. A Methodist bishop in North America has said that the history of the church has a long list of ministers who fell into sexual sin thinking they were the exception to the rule. Such ministers say that, though others got into trouble through such relationships, this one is different. But suddenly it has gone too far. Good people have been hurt and become the subject of scandalous stories. God is dishonored and effective ministries are ruined.

We may delude ourselves into thinking that nothing harmful is happening, but our friends may see its harm. They may notice that something more than normal friendship is developing. It may be the way the eyes of two people meet. It may be the amount of time spent together. Or it may simply be the way they talk to each other. An observant person will sense that the relationship is going too far. The friends' words of warning could open the endangered persons' eyes to see the real situation and avoid so many woes.

Sadly, however, some people see these things happening and do nothing because they think it is none of their business. Even worse is the common practice, when people see or hear about such things, of gossiping about it without talking to the people involved. This is selfish and alien to the Christian model of concern for the welfare of others.

Friends being advised may resent the type of involvement in their affairs we are advocating. Leaders especially find it difficult to take advice in this way. They are so used to giving advice that they are unaccustomed to being advised. A survey of medical doctors once revealed that preachers were among the hardest people to treat. They seem to think they know everything, which makes it difficult for doctors to get them to follow advice! Let us discipline ourselves to take the advice of others seriously. We need others to show us when we are headed in the wrong direction.

## Becoming Wise People

Proverbs 19:20 says, "Listen to advice and accept instruction, and in the end you will be wise." Robert Alden says that this "might be called the key verse of the book because it neatly summarizes what Proverbs is all about." This verse is talking about a process. It is in the end that the person becomes wise. We are not born wise. There are no short cuts to wisdom. Wisdom comes as the reward of applying oneself to knowledge.

Sometimes we are filled with admiration for a good writer. We observe that just the right words seem to flow from her pen. Her free and easy-to-read style suggests she has not labored long and hard with communication. But if you asked this writer what makes her writing so fine, she would invariably say she struggled to use just the right word, especially in her early years as a writer. Her dynamic style is the product of a process that included hard work and patient revising and re-revising. Those early struggles helped stamp a dynamic writing style into her being.

Wisdom comes to us in similar fashion. It is not always easy to accept advice. But those who conscientiously submit themselves to the discipline of being advised by others will in the end be wise. And what a wonderful quality wisdom is! Wisdom is worth all the humiliation of acting as a learner when others confidently paraded themselves as experts. The "experts" remained where they were. They did not think they needed to learn. The humble learners, on the other hand, did not look too confident in the crowd. But their commitment to learning helped them keep climbing so that, at the end, they had reached heights "confident" people could never hope to reach.

## *Beyond Receiving Advice*

Some persons think they are so knowledgeable they no longer need advice. Proverbs 19:27 says, "Stop listening to instruction, my son, and you will stray from the words of knowledge." Derek Kidner titles this proverb "Trifling with truth." Such persons have become careless, perhaps due to overconfidence.

This type of carelessness can hit us after we have achieved some success. People say, "You were great." And we believe them. But it is not true. Our preaching or our performance at our job or on the playing field may have been great. But there's more to life than preaching or a job or the playing field. Life involves family life, thought life, devotional life, and study life. Often we think that because we have done well in one area we are good in every area. But that is not true.

Because of our sense of achievement, we can become careless and stray from God's will. Our success muffles the questionings of our actions by the Spirit through our consciences. Because we have climbed so high, no one challenges our actions and feeds our souls with spiritual food. Some top leaders have no one to whom they are spiritually accountable. They have boards to guide their policy decisions. They have consultants who advise them on technical matters. But no one advises them on their day-to-day work.

True friends deflate the false bubble of success we may have around us. They know us too well to put us on a pedestal. They know weaknesses not often seen in public. They help us come down to reality and realize we are just ordinary people.

But sometimes the fall from cloud nine is agonizing. Here is a person who has just delivered a brilliant speech to a prestigious gathering. Many people praise him after the speech. Talking to them makes him late coming home. His wife has asked him to get food for the family on the way back from the meeting. Basking in the glow of praise, he forgets all about the food. Because he is late, the children are hungry, restless, and hence a strain on their mother's nerves. She meets her husband at the door and inquires first not about the speech but about the food.

He is jolted back to reality. His success as an orator did not immunize him from failure as a husband and father. He could snap back at his wife and say that the "great" work of speaking to 1000 people caused him to forget the "little" family chore. But in God's sight greatness is not determined by the size of the audience! Parenting is also great work.

Is this why so many marriages are ruined when one spouse achieves great success? Say the husband succeeds. This was what the wife longed for. They struggled to make ends meet during their early years of marriage. She dreamed of the day her husband would be rich and famous. Now that dream is fulfilled. But she does not recognize this new husband. He now lives in the unreal world of success and fame.

People who succeed in public life need close friends who will help them avoid the perils of success. If they are married, their spouses are the best people to help them come down to earth. This will help them avoid the moral failures that have marred the lives of so many Christian leaders.

# SEVEN

# *The Wounds of a Friend*

The last chapter showed that giving advice is not always pleasant. In fact Proverbs says one of a friend's roles is to wound. This is so important that we will devote a whole chapter to it.

## *Wounds Versus Flattery*

Proverbs 27:5-6 says, "Better is open rebuke than hidden love. Wounds from a friend can be trusted, but an enemy multiplies kisses." Friends must sometimes wound us because they love us. This happens when they observe our weaknesses and errors. They are responsible to rebuke us.

But wounds hurt, and we are so afraid of pain that we sometimes prefer the kisses of an enemy. There is a charge here to consider the source of a statement and sometimes let the source override our immediate feelings about the statement. That is, if a friend has wounded us, we should not immediately dismiss the wounding as an unkind act. It may be a blessing in disguise.

But being honest can be painful and risky for the one doing the wounding. That is why Proverbs 27:6 describes it as "wounds from a friend." For a time we will really suffer from the consequences of doing it. We will appear unkind and unappreciative, perhaps judgmental and even jealous. But in the long run, the risk will prove worthwhile. Proverbs 28:23 says, "He who rebukes a man will in the end gain more favor." When persons realize they were wrong and the friends who rebuked them were right, they will—if they have any integrity—thank the rebuker.

I have a colleague, Tony, who is well known for frankness. But he is also known for faithfulness to his friends. Because of this many go to him for counsel. Because of his nontraditional approach to life, many so-called way out youth are not hesitant to befriend Tony. But because of his frankness, he has infuriated many. Tony is not the type of person everyone calls a nice guy. Yet it is significant that when people he has infuriated are in trouble or realize that they have been wrong after all, Tony is often the first one they go to for help. Then they appreciate his honesty.

I must hasten to add that there is a time and a place for rebuking. Rebuking is not simply a thing we do mechanically without considering its effects. A valid rebuke can do more harm than good if done at the wrong time and place. Generally I try to avoid rebuking a person publicly. But if a person's error has had a deep impact on others, we may have to make a public rebuke. Paul told Timothy that elders "who sin are to be rebuked publicly, so that the others may take warning" (1 Tim. 5:20). However, we usually need not unnecessarily humiliate a person by public rebuke.

I have also learned that it may be good to wait for a time after someone has finished an emotionally draining activity before we criticize the activity. For many people preaching is emotionally draining. Most preachers are encouraged by compliments given them after a sermon. If a preacher has not done well and it would help him to hear where he failed, it may be better to wait until the emotional exhaustion from the event has died down. Otherwise he could overreact to the wound, becoming overly discouraged. He may be too tired emotionally at this time to take the blow. But we do not need to compliment him, which would be a lie. We can simply keep quiet and await a more opportune moment.

On the other hand, sometimes we may need to point out a shortcoming at an awkward moment to save a person from repeating the mistake. This happened to me at one of our English-language Youth for Christ evangelistic camps. These camps are a real challenge to me, as I have to battle to win the attention and interest of the Westernized youth, many of whom know little of Christianity and are not interested in religious matters. As most of my ministry is with youth who are culturally more Eastern, I was particularly nervous as I spoke to this group.

I was giving a two-part series on the life of Christ. About half an hour before the second talk, Tony, my colleague of whom I spoke earlier, came into the dormitory where I was nervously making last minute preparations. He had met a short while before with youth leaders at the camp for their daily evaluation session. He brought me the news that my first talk had gone over the heads of some youth.

It may seem inappropriate that he told me this half an hour before I was to speak. But Tony's warning told me I needed to do some fresh thinking about how to communicate more simply. I discarded my elaborate notes and hastily worked out a modified outline using the material in the notes. I added new illustrations. Then I pleaded for help from God and rushed to the meeting hall.

The reports I received of the second talk were that I communicated much better. How grateful I was to Tony that he was bold enough to tell me about the response to my first talk even though the timing seemed wrong. It takes commitment to do such things.

How do we know when and when not to tell people of their flaws? That is a decision we have to make after weighing pros and cons of the different options before us. The lesson that emerges from the example of Tony is that we must approach our conversations with a serious resolve to please God and help our friends. It is a serious thing to wound friends. But we may have to do that for their good and God's glory.

People who take relationships lightly will abstain from wounding because they do not want to face the consequences. Or they will simply say what comes to mind without making sure that what they are going to say is correct and that this is the best time to say it.

In contemporary society, people are used to taking lightly matters not relating to their self-fulfillment. It is troublesome to worry too much about other people. So they take a careless approach to their relationships. The only thing they take seriously is selfishness! These people save themselves a lot of trouble, for wounding a friend *is* hard. But they don't see that the way of self-denial for the sake of others, the way of the cross, is the only means to a deeply satisfying and liberated life. Because they don't pay the price of friendship, they don't experience the joys of friendship.

Proverbs 27:6 says that "an enemy multiplies kisses." We may call these unkind kisses. In this verse we have kind wounding contrasted with unkind kissing. A common form of this unkind kissing is flattery. And, as we saw, a common type of wounding is the rebuke. These two are found together in Proverbs 28:23 which says, "He who rebukes a man will in the end gain more favor than he who has a flattering tongue."

Flattery is dangerous. But it has become so common we do not think much of its consequences. Proverbs 29:5 says, "Whoever flatters his neighbor is spreading a net for his feet." Flattery is like a trap we can fall into. It makes us feel so good. But we may be feeling good about something that is wrong or needs to be changed. This is why flattery is so unkind. When we could be helping persons, we are harming them. Better to have said nothing.

## Wounds That Increase Understanding
Proverbs 15:31-32 says that rebuke and correction help us to become wise. "He who listens to a life-

giving rebuke will be at home among the wise. He who ignores discipline despises himself, but whoever heeds correction gains understanding."

Christians who take their walk with God seriously will soon realize that wisdom is a treasure. Our great desire in life is to do God's will. But it is not always clear what God's will is. There are so many decisions to make, so many voices crying for attention, so many challenges before us, so many problems to solve.

We are confronted all the time with questions: What should I commit myself to? Whom should I support with my prayers, gifts, and time? How can I stop this person from exploiting me? How do I know whether this "opening" is a trap of Satan or an opportunity provided by God? What advice can I give this person who has come to me for help? How should I respond to this neighbor whose behavior so taxes my patience? How can I motivate this discouraged colleague?

These challenges all call for wisdom. No wonder Proverbs says so much about the value of wisdom. Here is a passage that exults at the value of wisdom.

> Blessed is the man who finds wisdom, the man who gains understanding, for she is more profitable than silver and yields better returns than gold. She is more precious than rubies; nothing you desire can compare with her. Long life is in her right hand; in her left hand are riches and honor. Her ways are pleasant ways, and all her paths are peace. She is a tree of life to those who embrace her; those who lay hold of her will be blessed (Prov. 3:13-18).

If wisdom is so valuable, we will pay a big price to procure it. Proverbs 15:31-32 tells us that often this price is the wounding or rebuking of a friend. We should be deeply grateful to a friend who, through rebuke, helps us increase our understanding. It is painful at the time, just as it is painful for an Olympic gold medalist when his coach sends him through a rigorous training schedule before the Olympic games. With the gold medal in his possession, he will glow with praise for his coach. Wise people realize wisdom is more important even than a gold medal. So they are grateful to friends who faithfully rebuked.

## Fools

If the rebukes of friends do so much good to us, then it is not surprising that Proverbs has strong words about those who dislike being rebuked. Proverbs 12:1 says, "Whoever loves discipline loves knowledge, but he who hates correction is stupid." *Stupid* is a strong word! But that's what the NIV uses here. Obviously it is intended to have a strong effect on the reader. Such is needed because we often flee the pain of correction. We like to avoid looking stupid when our errors come to light. But here we are told that such an understanding of stupidity is what is actually stupid.

Proverbs 13:18 tells us a reason why such thinking is stupid. "He who ignores discipline comes to poverty and shame, but whoever heeds correction is honored." One who does not take advice seriously will persist in his errors. These will lead to his downfall. I've seen bright people with tremendous potential lose their effectiveness because they did not heed advice.

Let's take an example. An evangelist decides to set up a hospital as part of his ministry. He believes the hospital will pay for itself through fees charged when it is in operation. But the experts tell him there are sufficient hospital beds in the region; therefore he will have difficulty keeping the new hospital going. They advise him against the project. He still builds the hospital. After a few years the hospital becomes a heavy drain on his ministry. And he has to spend a lot of time and energy raising money to keep it going. He is distracted from his primary calling as evangelist. He did not listen to advice and was saddled with a big burden.

We need visionaries in the kingdom. But without advisers, they can make big mistakes. With the help of advisers, their visions will take workable forms. The practical people may modify the plans here and there. But the result will be much better plans than the ones originally dreamed up by the visionary. As plans are put into operation and achieve so much good for the kingdom, the visionary, who allowed the plans to be moderated by the practical people, "is honored" (13:18) for the achievement.

The end product of heeding correction is honor. Billy Graham tells of advice a senior Christian leader gave him early in his ministry after he had preached an evangelistic sermon. The leader told Graham that whenever he preached an evangelistic message, he should proclaim the cross of Christ. That ingredient of the gospel had been missing in the message Graham had just given. It is not easy for a preacher to accept such correction so soon after preaching. But Graham took the advice and has now preached the message of the cross for decades. And God has honored Billy Graham's preaching.

This then is the logic of Proverbs 13:18. "He who ignores discipline comes to poverty and shame, but whoever heeds correction is honored."

There are other sobering verses in Proverbs that talk of the severe consequences of not heeding correction. They don't need much comment. Their vivid language is comment enough. Proverbs 15:10 says, "He who hates correction will die." And 29:1 says, "A man who remains stiff-necked after many rebukes will suddenly be destroyed—without remedy."

## Teachable People

If hating correction is stupidity, then willingness to learn from others is the key aspect of wisdom. It is therefore not surprising that Proverbs presents teachability as a high virtue. Proverbs 23:12 says, "Apply your heart to instruction and your ears to words of knowledge." This verse tells us to be eager to learn.

Proverbs 17:10 places the emphasis on the more unpleasant aspect of teachability, the openness to be rebuked. "A rebuke impresses a man of discernment more than a hundred lashes a fool" (see also 13:1).

Some people are not very teachable because they try to protect an image that they are mature or learned. They build walls around themselves, and their minds are difficult to penetrate, especially when someone wants to address their faults. The Bible, on the other hand, has much to say about the value of soft hearts easily penetrated by God's Spirit and Christians who are agents of the Spirit.

This openness to penetration by the Spirit is the essence of teachability. Robert Alden's comment on 17:10 is worth quoting here: "People who are wise are also sensitive; their consciences are tender and their wills are pliant."

This softness is a key to holiness and is itself the mark of a true work of the Spirit in a person's life. Such softness will be a characteristic of the restored Israel spoken of in Ezekiel 36:26-27: "I will give you a new heart and put a new spirit in you; I will remove from you your heart of stone and give you a heart of flesh. And I will put my Spirit in you and move you to follow my decrees."

The great feature of a heart of flesh is that it can be penetrated by God. As Charles Bridges puts it, "A needle pierces deeper into flesh than a sword into stone." It is not difficult to correct those who are sensitive to God. If they are in the wrong, they accept their mistake and do what is necessary to right the wrong.

In our work with Youth for Christ, we have many young full-time and volunteer staff. Some of them, filled with a lot of zeal and sometimes insufficient wisdom, make mistakes that may even have some bad effects on our work and reputation. This is something we have come to accept as necessary difficulty of working with youth. Despite the damage to the work, we do not view these mistakes as very serious. But sometimes when errors are pointed out, we find those at fault unwilling to accept responsibility. We see that as a serious problem, for it may indicate lack of the teachable spirit. Commenting on Proverbs 17:10, Charles Bridges says, "Reproof distinguishes the wise man from the fool."

Thus when we select staff for our work, key qualities we look for are teachability or soft-heartedness. Teachability is a quality that cannot be gauged from an interview or a written application. Generally it is those who have moved closely with applicants who know this. If applicants have not been accountable to a group, we are wary of accepting them on staff, however talented they may be. This is because their lack of practice at accountability may indicate lack of teachability.

The usual way to reject a rebuke is to give another explanation for the alleged error. Christians often give explanations and excuses that are not quite true. Often Christian leaders, not wanting the unpleasantness and pain of confrontation, accept the explanation without fully believing it. That is irresponsible.

A false excuse or explanation for a sin is more serious than the sin itself. Nowhere in the Bible is it said that we are immune to sin. The Bible says over and over that there is hope of healing for those who confess their sin. But those who don't accept that they have sinned have no hope. These principles are most clearly taught in 1 John 1:5—2:2. This familiar passage says there is hope for healing and fellowship with fellow Christians for those who walk in the light. The context shows that a key aspect of walking in the light is willingness to accept and confess one's sin.

What we have said, then, is that people who benefit from a rebuke are those who, having a soft heart, accept responsibility for error. They learn from their mistakes. They receive God's forgiveness so God's grace is not blocked from coming into their lives. Their futures are bright with the endless, exciting possibilities of God's rich grace.

How can hard hearts become soft? How can those accustomed to lying overcome the temptation to give an incorrect excuse or explanation for their error? Is not lying one of the habits hardest to overcome? Looking at the lack of integrity we see in the church today, we may be filled with despair.

But the passage we cited from Ezekiel gives us hope. We may not be able to develop soft hearts. But God can give us such hearts. Ezekiel 36:26 says, "*I will* give you a new heart, and put a new spirit within you; *I will* remove from you your heart of stone and give you a heart of flesh" (emphasis added). This is God speaking! What we cannot do God can do in us.

The agent God often uses in creating in us a clean heart of integrity is the community of believers. As 1 John 1:7 points out, those who walk in the light have fellowship with one another. The converse of this is also true. Those who do not walk in the light cannot have fellowship with one another. If the community of believers is truly biblical, then those not willing to face their sin will soon feel out of place. They must change and start walking in the light or leave the community. Praise God, the history of the church has many examples of people who stayed on and changed.

Lack of integrity is a major problem in the church today. It is difficult to know who is truthful and who is not. If biblical community life is practiced, you will find out. Those without integrity will either change or leave.

How alien teachability is in our society, where so

much effort is made to put on a big show! The truly great people are always aware of how little they know. They learn from anyone and admit it. They accept their faults and are grateful when rebuked. This is because their aim in life in relation to this world is not to show how smart they are. They are followers of a servant Lord. Their aim is to serve. They are therefore grateful when a hindrance to effective service is pointed out.

Evangelist D. L. Moody was fond of gardening and proud of his flower beds in his home in Chicago. One day when he came home he found that his sons had romped on his flower beds and destroyed their beauty. Infuriated, he reprimanded his children severely. Afterward, the children went up to their rooms. Eventually they heard their father coming up. The stairs were wooden and Moody was heavy, so there was no doubt in the children's minds that the sound was that of their father coming up. "Now what?" they thought to themselves.

What their father said not only allayed their fears but also left a marked impression on them. He did not condone their error, but he confessed his own error in overreacting and losing his temper. He asked their forgiveness. Here was the most prominent evangelist and possibly the most famous Christian in the church in the West in his day. But he did not shrink from admitting his wrong and asking the forgiveness of his children. That is a mark of one whose great desire in life is to fear God. No wonder God used him in such a powerful way that even now, almost ninety years after his death, the church is still enjoying the fruits of his labors.

When we describe teachability we are not referring to the mentality of professional students who spend all their time studying, just for the sake of studying. Teachable people learn so they can put into practice what they learn. The end of our knowledge is obedience and service. And the end of obedience and service is the glory of God, not teachability. Our primary ambition is not to be teachable; it is to be Christlike and to bring glory to God!

Some supposedly teachable people don't launch out on any project for God. They are not qualified, they say. That also is not true teachability. The refusal to launch out on fresh exploits for God often comes from pride. Some people don't try something new because they are reluctant to make mistakes and so make fools of themselves. Sometimes this reluctance comes from laziness. These people simply don't want to stretch themselves to launch out on new and difficult ventures.

Biblical teachability comes out of burning desire to see God glorified by our lives and actions. Our passion for God's glory gives us strength to face the humiliation of accepting our faults. Our aim is not to show our abilities to the world. It is to show God's abilities. We gladly accept any help we can get to glorify God, even if we must endure being humbled.

# EIGHT

# Friendship and Uncontrolled Tongues

We have in this book encountered some factors that can destroy friendships. Proverbs specifically mentions many instances where friendships can be destroyed by the uncontrolled use of the tongue. In this chapter we will look at some of these sins of the tongue.

### Insincere Words

The first text we will study describes insincere words. Proverbs 27:14 says, "If a man loudly blesses his neighbor early in the morning, it will be taken as a curse." This verse has been understood in two ways. Since I find it difficult to decide between the two I will describe both.

*Inconsiderate helpfulness.* The first interpretation is to take the act of blessing ones neighbor early in the morning as an example of inconsiderate behavior. R. B. Y. Scott suggests that the reference to the blessing being given loudly may imply that the blessing roused the neighbor in the morning (presumably from sleep). According to this interpretation the blessing was imposed on the person in a way that became a hindrance, or as the proverb says, "a curse," to the one being blessed. In our eagerness to do what we believe is right, we must not forget that the right thing must be done lovingly and in a sensitive way.

Let me list some examples of inconsiderate blessing. A young man is about to give his first major sermon before an august assembly. He has worked hard on the sermon and almost memorized it. Just before the service starts, a friend who knows the sermon topic comes up to our preacher and gives him a dose of his great insight. All this eloquent speech does is confuse the nervous, novice preacher. Even if the ideas are excellent, it is too late for him to include them in his carefully prepared sermon.

A young woman is going to a foreign country for higher studies. A friend wants to give her a parting gift. She knows that at this time the person going abroad needs money. The friend also knows the student's bag must not weigh over forty pounds. But the friend decides not to give money because such a gift will not be remembered. So the friend gets a framed painting and asks the student to take it abroad as a memento of their friendship. The gift was selfish, for it added significantly to the weight of the bag.

An elderly person gets a heart attack in the middle of a church service. As they are rushing him to a hospital, a Christian worker stops them and says she wants to pray for this unconscious person. She delays them even though she could easily have said the same prayer without stopping the rush to the hospital.

An all-night prayer meeting is being held in the home of a sick person. A main item of prayer is for the healing of this person. But the people pray so loudly they keep awake the sick person, who desperately needs sleep.

These are examples of blessings that become curses, as our proverb says, because they are given insensitively. This can happen when our service becomes an expression of our selfishness. We get satisfaction from the service, so we do it regardless of whether the person needs it or the time and place is appropriate.

Let me give an example of a "blessing" withheld by a person out of sensitivity and who gave a greater blessing by not offering the original one. Two theological students went one Sunday to minister in a church far from their theological school. Both were good preachers who later became prominent Christian leaders.

The plan that Sunday was for one student to give a five-minute testimony and the other to preach a full-length sermon in the morning service. In the evening service, they would reverse roles. The morning service went as planned. But at the evening service the preacher of the morning, now giving his testimony, got carried away. His testimony grew as long as a sermon and was powerful.

The preacher rose to preach after special music

which followed the testimony. He sensed that the powerful testimony and song had made a marked impression on the people. It would be more appropriate to give an invitation to discipleship than to preach his prepared sermon. He did this in five minutes. Many people came to the altar to commit their lives to Christ. He could not "bless" the people with his preaching, but God gave them a much richer blessing!

Those who are inconsiderate in helping people will find it difficult to establish and keep close friendships. A selfish streak enters their relationships with others. This makes it difficult for them to open themselves to the self-giving which is a basic ingredient in a friendship relationship. In fact, because these inconsiderate "helpers" impose themselves on others, people avoid them to escape the unwanted help.

*Insincere expressions of concern.* The second way to interpret this proverb is to understand it as addressing insincere expression of concern. Charles Bridges presents this view well. "When a man exceeds all bounds of truth and decency, affecting pompous words and hyperbolical expressions, we cannot but suspect some sinister end."

The underlying idea in this interpretation is that we should be suspicious of exaggerated shows of friendship—which may hide sinister motives. The insincere friend may be trying to achieve selfish goals. For example, hopes of eventual profit, not true friendship, are what lie behind business gifts given to prospective clients.

Sometimes a big show of friendship hides the true shallowness of the relationship. As Bridges says, "Real friendship needs no such assurance." My mother once told us about an interesting thing that happened when she went to a function in Sri Lanka many decades ago. This was in the days when couples never expressed affection to each other in public. There she saw a married couple give a public show of affection. A few weeks later the couple had separated and were soon divorced. The unusual show of affection was probably an attempt to hide a troubled relationship.

How do these insincere expressions of concern become a curse, as the verse claims? A sad quality of most of us is believing nice things said about us and attributing pure motives to them. "At least he understands me," we say. This way we may believe in a falsehood and act on it. We trust people because we confuse the good feelings their words create in our minds with trustworthiness. We act on that trust and only later find out we have been deceived and snared in an unscrupulous scheme. None of us are immune to vanity; we become vulnerable when people pander to it.

Unscrupulous people can, through cunning, win partners for their devious schemes. But they cannot win true friends. Honesty is a basic requirement for real friendship, and they lack it.

## Gossip

Gossip is one of the most serious sins of the tongue. Gossip is mentioned often in Proverbs in connection with what it does to friendships.

*Friendships broken.* Gossip can break friendships. By gossiping people can lose their own friends and also destroy the friendships of others. Proverbs talks of both ways of separating friends.

Proverbs 17:9 says, "Whoever repeats the matter [of an offense committed by someone] separates close friends" (We will discuss this verse in the next chapter under the heading "Covering Offenses."). We can talk to others about mistakes a friend makes only because we are close to the friend. Upon learning of our gossip, our friend will feel betrayed. This is a sure way to lose friendship. We have shown by our actions that we do not really care for our friend. We are willing to humiliate our friend in exchange for the perverse thrill of gossiping. This disqualifies us from friendship.

Proverbs 16:28 seems to suggest that the gossip monger can break the friendship of two other people. "A perverse man stirs up dissension, and a gossip separates close friends." Let me describe how this happens. Sharon and Michelle are good friends. Peter, the gossip monger, tells Sharon that Michelle has told something nasty about Sharon. Sharon is so affected by this news that she feels she cannot trust Michelle any more. Their friendship is broken because of what Peter told Sharon.

Such gossip is a common cause of ill will in the body of Christ. The ill will usually happens in one of three ways. Perhaps most often it takes place *when people talk too much*. There is usually no malicious intention behind this gossiping. Some people have not learned to control their tongues. They have heard something. They may not even be sure of the facts. But they talk about it without thinking much about the accuracy and the appropriateness of what they are saying. They are speech addicts who cannot control the habit of talking.

While there may be no malicious intent behind this, it is a sign of a spiritual malady. Jesus said, "Out of the overflow of his heart his mouth speaks" (Luke 6:45). What comes out of your mouth is an indication of the health of your inner being. When gossip comes out it means there is a need for more of the beauty of Jesus to become part of you.

Let me suggest three ways to overcome this type of gossip. First, because gossiping is a sign of inner ugliness, we need to feed our minds with the beauty of Christ. Paul's advice in Philippians 4:8 is appropriate. "Whatever is true, whatever is noble, whatever is right, whatever is pure, whatever is lovely, whatever is admirable—if anything is excellent or praiseworthy—think about such things."

Inner beauty is not formed in us overnight. We must linger with God's Word so God's thoughts can fill our beings. We must be sure our minds do not have the cancer of hate and the spirit of unforgiveness which destroy beauty. Such attitudes must be surrendered to God and his help enlisted in our pursuit of Christlikeness.

Second, we need to be conscious of our gossip problem and be on guard lest our tongues slip into the old habit. However much time we spend with God, we live in a fallen world; ill will is in our environment. It is so easy to win a hearing with gossip. Even when Christian leaders meet, gossip will generally interest everyone present. A key text can bring much beauty to the life of the church: "Set a guard over my mouth, O Lord, keep watch over the door of my lips" (Ps. 141:3).

Third, when we realize we have spoken out of turn

we should go to God, ask forgiveness, and do all we can to right the wrong. We may need to write letters asking the persons who heard us to forgive us for polluting their mind and appeal to them to try to erase the dirt from their mind. We may visit the people we spoke to with the same intention. This step suggests that we are serious about the problem. It is a sure remedy. God honors such seriousness of purpose. The inconvenience of going through this long process of restitution will deter further gossip.

What I have said above is basic. Yet the problem of gossip continues to cause havoc among Christians. Often those guilty of gossip are respected leaders. It is clear that Christians are not grappling adequately with this issue. Therefore it would be good to upgrade, or should we say downgrade, gossip to the status of being a major problem in the church.

*Immature loyalty* is another factor which feeds gossip. For example, a young Christian loyal to his leader hears that a friend of the leader has said something bad about the leader. Because of his loyalty to his leader, the young Christian rushes to her and relates the incident. "This is what your friend said about you," he says. This places the leader in a difficult position. She cannot erase the report from her mind. Ideally she should check with her friend whether this is true. But sometimes she may be hindered from doing this because she and her friend are already experiencing tension. Usually it is when there is tension between leaders that loyal people relate such stories to their leaders. Then the cleavage is widened. And the process of healing is made so much harder.

Christians who tell such gossip must learn it is wrong. They should talk to the person who made the statement against the leader before going to the leader. That would save much unnecessary heartache.

The third way gossip takes place is *out of malice*. This is a different form of the gossip from the first two, which are devoid of serious intent to harm.

A good way to describe those who gossip maliciously is to contrast them with those who do not do this. Those who avoid gossip are overwhelmed by gratitude to God. Their gratitude helps a sweetness of disposition become part of their nature. They are so grateful for the way that God has been good to them that now they gladly give their energy to bringing some of the love they have experienced to others.

These are the people whose fulfillment in life comes from God. The love of God has removed bitterness and replaced it with gratitude for healing grace. They may be people who have a lot of problems, but they have found that God's grace is sufficient to face the pain of their troubles. Such people are not angry with the world. And so they won't harm people.

But many people, even in the church, have not let the grace of God heal their hurts. They approach life with anger—anger over the way they have been treated. This anger finds an outlet in gossip. They get fulfillment from saying bad things about people. Their anger against people who have hurt them is unleashed in unkind words said about others.

Sometimes when angry or frustrated, children express their satisfaction over another's misfortune. One of my now famous angry statements as a child was: "It was very good that Mr. Menzies fell off the chair." Mr. Menzies was my aunt's piano teacher. One day, during a piano lesson, the chair he was seated on broke and he fell, much to the embarrassment of my grandparents, at whose house this happened. I had nothing at all against Mr. Menzies. But it was an unfortunate incident, and in my angry condition I found expressing my satisfaction a good way to vent frustration.

Adults don't usually say such silly things. But they do something similar—they gossip. They vent their anger over the way people have treated them by saying bad things about others.

Malicious gossipers have an even more serious spiritual problem than those who gossip because they haven't learned to control their tongues. When Christians see other Christians do this, they need to approach the gossipers and talk about it with a view to being agents of healing.

***Betraying confidence.*** One type of gossip is singled out in Proverbs—sharing with others things a friend has shared in confidence. Proverbs 11:13 says, "A gossip betrays a confidence, but a trustworthy man keeps a secret." Proverbs 20:19 says, "A gossip betrays a confidence; so avoid a man who talks too much."

A person who keeps a secret is honorable. Honorable people will not break confidence, even if they have to pay a big price to remain silent. Proverbs 25:9-10 gives an instance of this. "If you argue your case with a neighbor, do not betray another man's confidence, or he who hears it may shame you and you will never lose your bad reputation." When you are in a tight spot in a court case you may be able to clear yourself by sharing something told you in confidence. Proverbs says you must not use this method even if you suffer from such refusal.

Christian leaders often encounter this problem. If they are proper leaders, they will know many things about those in their group which cannot be shared in public. Often in a conversation, the point may come when sharing these things would help to enlighten those who are there. But we must strenuously resist the temptation.

Perhaps the worst way to break a confidence is to talk about a secret in a sermon. However appropriate an incident may be in illustrating a point, we must not use it if this will break a confidence. We may sometimes use a story by modifying it so a person's identity is not revealed. For example, I may speak of an experience I had as if it happened to someone else. I may start like this: "A young man came to a Christian minister with this problem. . . ." The audience does not know I am the minister. Some details of the story can be modified, so it becomes a parable based on fact. A story which can't be modified in this way should not be used.

David Seamands dealt with this problem well in his book *Healing for Damaged Emotions*, where he used illustrations from his counseling ministry. But he first got permission from those about whom he was going to write. Then he changed their names and held back other details that might allow readers to identify those being written about.

*Avoid gossips*. Proverbs 20:19 asks us to avoid those who betray a confidence. "A gossip betrays a confidence; so avoid a man who talks too much." Gossips not only separate friends, they separate themselves from their own friends. Their insatiable desire to talk makes them share confidences. Friends of gossips do not trust them, and they leave the friendship. True friendships include sharing confidential matters, but the gossips have shown themselves unable to handle the responsibility of keeping secrets. Thus they forfeit the right to hear confidential matters.

What an irony this is! People who talk too much end up not having anyone to involve in conversation that really matters to them—the affirming conversations that friends have with each other. This is what banishes our loneliness and brings us the great blessings friendship offers. The irony is that gossips indulge in gossip to have someone listen to them. They may get listeners, but they won't get what they need—friends. They may get malicious satisfaction from winning a hearing through unsavory talk. But because they act against God's way for a fulfilled life, their misery and loneliness are compounded.

Proverbs 18:8 advises us to avoid gossip mongers because gossip can have a strong influence upon us. "The words of a gossip are like choice morsels; they go down to a man's inmost parts" (the same proverb appears again in 26:22). The words of a gossip are described as "choice morsels." Most people like to hear a juicy story about someone. As Robert Alden comments, "The point is gossip seems so 'delicious' to us that we are powerless to resist it." In fact, one who gossips is generally sure to win a hearing.

Our eagerness to hear destructive rumors is a sign

of our fallenness. It gives us a certain satisfaction to know others are sinners. It temporarily soothes our insecurity. But this is sinful and unloving. As Paul says, "Love does not delight in evil" (1 Cor. 13:6). Of course, the security rumors give is fleeting. True security comes from knowing we have been forgiven in Christ, considered righteous, and accepted as full members of the family of God.

Proverbs 18:8 and 26:22 not only say that the words of a gossip taste delicious, they also say that these words "go down to a man's inmost parts." Kenneth Aitken explains this statement clearly.

> Once digested the whisperer's words are never quite forgotten. They remain indelibly imprinted on the mind. So while the hearer might keep it to himself, the very fact that he heard means the damage has been done; for thereafter his attitude to and relationship with the whisperer's victim will never quite be the same.

Because of these lasting effects of gossip, good people learn to leave the scene when a gossip talks. In fact, Proverbs says that to deliberately listen to such tales is wicked. Proverb 17:4 says, "A wicked man listens to evil lips; a liar pays attention to a malicious tongue." With those strong words from Proverbs, we will end this section, reminding readers that uncontrolled tongues disqualify people from friendship and greatly dishonor God.

## Confronting Sins of the Tongue

The Scriptures give an important place to the havoc caused by the unsanctified use of the tongue. Two books that focus on practical hints for daily life, Proverbs and James, have much to say about this. Therefore, Christians need to confront this issue. We should rebuke unsanctified use of the tongue.

Yet often Christians feel they don't have the freedom to confront another Christian for something like this. Generally, uncontrolled tongues are allowed to go unchecked and so cause much destruction. If we don't have the freedom to confront gossipers with the seriousness of their sin, that indicates the fellowship has moved far from the biblical model. If a church or some other fellowship in the body of Christ realizes it has come to this point, then it's time to get really serious with God. I have used the word *serious* many times in this chapter. This is because the church is, among other things, a community of people seriously intent on pleasing God.

Alas, many churches seem so influenced by the entertainment orientation of today's society that seriousness seems to have been eclipsed by the desire to somehow keep the Christians satisfied by giving them an enjoyable time. Leaders are afraid that if they point out these errors some members will go to the church down the road.

In addition, often churches have not been serious enough about fellowship to develop an atmosphere conducive to confronting people about personal behavior. People come to church to get blessed and leave. Some members volunteer their services for some programs of the church. The leaders are grateful for this. And if the leaders confronted the servers, they might get upset and leave. So confrontation is avoided.

My point is that the church should be seriously addressing the sins that surface in its body life. And sins of the tongue surface often. Gossips must be made to feel uncomfortable with gossiping and at the same time showered with the holy care of reproof, counsel, and instruction that will help them kick the habit.

Sincere Christians won't leave a church that demonstrates true concern for them. In fact, such a church need not use entertainment to keep the crowd. If people know the church is truly committed to them, they reciprocate by being committed to the church. They stay, not because they are entertained, but because they have a sense of ownership. They are committed. Commitment can stand the test of painful experiences. In fact, when there is commitment, painful experiences serve to make the tie even deeper.

Again we come to the principle that costly commitment is not as unpragmatic as it seems. The results may take longer to come and the experiences are sometimes stretching. But what emerges is far more satisfying and lasting. The methods that have replaced commitment are no match for the real thing! They will leave the church impoverished and ineffective.

# NINE

# The Comfort of a Friend

The last two chapters were severe in dealing with wounding that is a part of friendship and the destruction of friendship through wrong use of the tongue. In this concluding chapter, it is appropriate to celebrate the glory of friendship.

## Covering Offenses

In an earlier chapter we said we are responsible to point out the faults of our friends, but we are also called to cover their offenses. Proverbs 17:9 says, "He who covers an offense promotes love, but whoever repeats the matter separates close friends." Similarly 10:12 says, "Love covers over all wrongs."

What does it mean to cover offenses? Other passages in Proverbs help us eliminate the idea that it means hushing up a person's sins or being reluctant to rebuke a person who does wrong. The Scriptures also tell us we must publicly rebuke persons, especially leaders, whose sins bring public dishonor to God (1 Tim. 5:20).

The antithesis of covering sin as presented in Proverbs 17:9 helps us understand covering sin. After mentioning the need to cover offenses, Proverbs says, "Whoever repeats the matter separates close friends." The two parallel statements in a Hebrew proverb are usually closely allied, as is true here. Repeating a matter is the opposite of covering a sin. To repeat a matter may mean either harping on it (as the New English Bible (NEB) understands it), or tale-telling (as most of the other translations I consulted understand it).

In both cases the root of the matter is the biblical understanding of forgiveness. Once a person has confessed a sin and received forgiveness, God no longer remembers the sin (Jer. 31:34). In the same way, we as followers of God's ways must forget sins that have been forgiven.

Before we can forget a sin, it must first be forgiven. That means the sin must be acknowledged by the wrongdoer and responsibility for it accepted. Otherwise there will be no forgiveness. And there can be no real fellowship either. First John 1:7 says, "If we walk in the light, as he is in the light, we have fellowship with one another." If a person refuses to walk in the light—which is what refusal to confess our sins is— then there can be no fellowship. But to those who will walk in the light the message of 1 John 1:7 is "the blood of Jesus, his Son, purifies us from all sin."

The sin of a person cleansed by the blood of Jesus

is forgotten. Then we who are servants of God must forget the sin too. This does not mean we are unaware of a person's weaknesses. It does mean we treat the person as if that thing was past. We don't bring it up in a way that damages the person.

I was once in a confrontation with a colleague. It was a necessary, though unpleasant, confrontation. I was not getting through. In an effort to press home my case, I referred to an issue settled many years before. That greatly complicated the current issue and made the resolution of the problem much more painful. I raised an unnecessary point to gain a quick but cheap advantage.

I praise the Lord that, because his grace was bigger than the problem, the resolution was complete and the ensuing unity deep as ever. But I learned an important lesson. We must not harp on sins that have been cleansed by the blood of Christ.

If harping on cleansed sins is a bad practice, talking about them to others is worse. This is betrayal of friendship. People often share confidential things with us about errors they have made and sins they have committed. As people love to hear gossip and we love to have people to listen to us speak, we may be tempted to share what was told us in confidence. Often this slips out of our mouths without much pre-planning.

What then does it mean to cover sin? We have seen that it means we must not talk about sin without a biblically-endorsed reason for doing so. But there may be more to this. Charles Martin suggests that covering sin means "keeping matters discreetly until reconciliation is achieved."

How often we bring private disagreements or opinions about the actions of people out into the public without first confronting the people directly. When we act too quickly, the chances of our being an influence for good in the situation are greatly reduced. We lose credibility by our hasty action.

So the action of covering sin has to do primarily with the control of our tongues. This is an area in which we must constantly do battle, however mature we may think we are. Our constant prayer should be: "Set a guard over my mouth, O Lord; keep watch over the door of my lips" (Ps. 141:3).

## When We Fall

Our next principle comes from a familiar passage on friendship in Ecclesiastes. "If one falls down, his friend can help him up. But pity the man who falls and has no one to help him up!" (Eccles. 4:10).

Michael Eaton points out that the background of this statement is a fall into a ditch or pit. "A lonely fall might be fatal, especially at night." Eaton goes on to say that "the proverb, however, looks beyond physical mishap" to "slips of judgment and other types of 'falling by the wayside.' "

*Discouragement after failure.* Failure makes us vulnerable to attacks which are sometimes worse than the failure itself. At such times friends are a great help in putting things in perspective. Failure can make us overly discouraged. Because you preached badly on one occasion, you may conclude preaching is something you are not called to do. Friends not emotionally devastated by the incident will knock some sense into you and show you the situation is not as bad as you think.

Friends may help you get sufficient courage to try again an exam you failed on your first attempt, or to keep singing even though your first solo was a disaster. I remember reading that the first public solo given by George Beverly Shea was terrible. But he did not give up singing. He went on to become one of the English-speaking world's best-loved gospel singers.

A more extreme form of over-discouragement is thinking that failure in one area makes you a failure in all of life. For example, because you lose a job, you might conclude you are worthless. At such times too your friends help you realize that life includes more than a job or whatever area you failed in. This gives courage to pick up the pieces of life and get a fresh start.

Hudson Taylor was a great missionary hero of the last century. Yet after being in China for a little less than two years, he was deeply discouraged. His missionary society had not kept its promise to support him. The established missionaries in China were critical of his unorthodox methods. His girlfriend in England had written that she feared she did not love him. The British consul had ordered him to stop work in one of the towns he was focusing on. He wrote to his mother, "My heart is sad, sad, sad. I do not know what to do."

At this stage a godly Scottish missionary named William Burns, about twenty years his senior, befriended Hudson Taylor. They traveled, preached, and prayed together for seven months. Burns was God's answer for Taylor's discouragement.

Nurtured by Burns, Taylor went on to found the China Inland Mission whose ministry over the years is one of the most exciting stories in missionary history. Eighty-three years after Taylor's death it still operates, though under a new name—Overseas Missionary Fellowship. Its old urgency to share Christ with the lost and its commitment to stick uncompromisingly to biblical principles continues to be a distinguishing mark of the movement.

Many Christians who launch out on difficult projects either give up or compromise their principles when they face the inevitable discouragement such ventures entail. We hear of missionaries who return home after a few years totally discouraged by their lack of visible fruit. Most of us know of Christians who have gone into fields often avoided by Christians, like politics and trade, and have compromised their Christian stands after a time.

But we also know of those who stick to their original commitments without compromising. Most of these people have other Christians to whom they are accountable and who encourage them along the path of obedience.

A classic example is William Wilberforce. As a member of the British parliament, he led a long campaign to abolish the slave trade in Britain. He experienced the joy of success only after many years. He suffered from frequent migraine attacks, possibly brought on by the strain of a bruising battle against slavery. But right through the battle he had a closely knit group of Christians, mostly members of his church in Clapham, who encouraged him, prayed for him, and mustered prayer support all over England for him.

There is a great need today for Christians to go into difficult professions—like reaching the unreached, secular journalism, law, politics, high school teaching, trade, social welfare, and finance and business. But those going into such professions face many obstacles and discouragements. It is dangerous to go into such work without the support of Christian friends. This is why I do not recommend sending workers alone to start a Christian work in a completely new area.

*In times of moral failure.* Friends are valuable in times of moral failure also. Many Christians struggle with moral problems they don't know how to solve. They are reluctant to tell just anyone about it. They are often caught in a trap of failure that keeps getting worse as time goes by. This is a particular problem with leaders, for they may not be able freely to share problems with just anyone.

The problem may be lust, or troubles may have developed in the relationship with one's spouse. It may be that people's devotions have gone dry, or that they are so busy with their job or ministry that they do not have time for family. If these problems are not dealt with, they can trap Christians in a descending spiral of defeat and discouragement. Soon they lose confidence in their ability to handle the problem. Others see them work hard at their job and think things are going fine in their life. Suddenly there is a big crash, such as a moral scandal or a divorce, and people are shocked and saddened.

When persons struggling with moral problems share with someone they trust, the usual immediate response is great relief. That relief itself may clear a lot of the air and take away the heavy load persons were living under. Now the strugglers can see their problems in more constructive ways. They may find out lust is something leaders are not immune to and learn ways to overcome lust. The accountability they have just affirmed with friends may be precisely what they needed to stop watching unedifying television programs or videocassettes. The fact that they have to report TV-watching to friends helps them resist the temptation to watch what they should not watch.

A simple word of advice a friend gives a struggling Christian may be all that is needed to help him snap back victoriously from the problem. For example, a young woman finds she is growing attracted to a married man who helps her in some way. She shares it with a friend whose advice gives her courage to take the difficult step of refusing the help. Once that step is taken, she quickly snaps back to her original state of spiritual vitality.

What we have said above underscores the importance of Paul's admonition in Galatians 6:1-2. "Brothers, if someone is caught in a sin, you who are spiritual should restore him gently. . . . Carry each other's burdens, and in this way you will fulfill the law of Christ."

## Spiritual Accountability Versus Superficial Fellowship

We must note that the context in which Ecclesiastes 4:10 appears (that is, verses 9-12) is that of describing people who work close to one another. Verse 9 speaks of those who have a good return for their work—that is, workmates. Verse 11 speaks of two who lie together —that is, a married couple or traveling mates who sleep close to one another to keep warm. Verse 12 speaks of two people who face an enemy together.

These verses suggest that those we live and work close to are the best people to provide us with the blessings of companionship. For married people, spouses will be important companions. Another level of sharing is with colleagues in ministry. They can form each other's accountability group.

However, there seems to be a trend among Christians toward forming accountability groups from people who are not close associates. Christians have business relationships with associates and sharing relationships with those in the accountability group. This again is a carryover into the church from a secular model of management.

Another trend we see is that people, lacking the blessing of spiritual accountability, are choosing shallow fellowship instead. Weekend retreats are popular in many countries. Here people share quite openly with strangers. There is value in this. Yet we must not confuse this with spiritual accountability. The fellowship is too shallow to be called accountability.

It is not easy to be frank with those with whom we work closely. It may slow down the work because time has to be spent clearing up barriers to being of one mind that would inevitably arise when people work close to each other. If we did not have such high expectations from the fellowship, we could ignore differences and go ahead with our work. Then we could do more work for the kingdom and be a more "successful" organization.

But such success is measured by a worldly standard. Success in the kingdom is determined by whether the work was done in God's way of doing ministry. The testimony of Scripture is surely that being "of one mind" is a necessary ingredient for a ministry team. (See Chapter Two, especially the section on "Friendship at Team Meetings.")

Our conclusion is that ministry teams that meet God's standards place a high emphasis on being of one mind. But clearing barriers to fellowship takes time and threatens the technical proficiency of the group. For example, practice time or sleep could get eaten into, leaving the team unprepared or tired during the program. But team members have, by paying that price, gained a spiritual power more capable than technical excellence of bearing eternal fruit.

Being spiritually accountable to your colleagues brings responsibility. When your accountability group is outside your immediate circle of colleagues, you can share your problems with the group, but you will not generally be challenged by the group. If, for example, you are doing something wrong which has caused a problem, you will invariably give the group your version of the problem, which may not be accurate. Based on that misinformation, your group may back you when they should be rebuking you!

If the problem is shared with people who work close to you, there is a greater chance of the group challenging you and helping you along the path to perfection. They will see if you are really making an effort to solve the problem. So your responsibility to share with those close to you is greater than your responsibility to those less close. Sharing is uncomfortable and humiliating at times. But that is the price of spiritual accountability.

Usually the accountability within "responsible" Christian organizations is confined to handling finances and the performance of duties in terms of job descriptions. Here we are making a plea to add the all-important aspect of spiritual accountability.

As in many spheres of activity, integrating the different facets of life is not easy. So we prefer to separate them. Therefore we have one group for spiritual accountability and another for vocational accountability. Bringing them together under one roof may cause friction. But from that friction comes ability to penetrate people deeply. Many of our shallow performances, despite their technical competence, fail to produce this ability truly to penetrate a people and a culture with the gospel of Christ.

## Warmth in Times of Need

Friends not only help us when we fall, they also bring the warmth of affirming concern when the cold realities of life in a hostile world hit us. The philosopher who wrote Ecclesiastes said, "If two lie down together, they will keep warm. But how can one keep warm alone?" (Eccles. 4:11).

As we have seen, this verse could refer to the husband-wife relationship. But more likely it refers to travelers who slept together in the cold winter nights of Israel in order to keep warm (Eaton). Unfortunately the rise of homosexuality in some cultures has made this type of activity seem somewhat unnatural. We have here a picture of companionship in times of adversity and grief. We are often battered by hostile forces. The cold realities of misunderstanding, opposition, grief, and failure often hit us with great intensity. What a comfort friends are at such times.

It is important to note again that the blessing of comfort described here is available to those who have a friend close enough to know what the problem is. I hear people complain that there is no one to help them through crises. They blame the church for not caring for them. Indeed the church should try to find out who is sick or in some difficulty among its fold. But often the reason the church does not know about problems is that sufferers have kept aloof and others have no way of finding out about their problems. They choose not to develop close friendships because that is too much of a nuisance. They preserve privacy, but miss the blessings of companionship.

Those who choose a lifestyle that includes cultivating close friendships and ministering in an open-hearted way with people become vulnerable to much inconvenience and pain. But when they face hardship, they usually find there are people willing to bear their burdens and help sacrificially. There may be exceptions to this rule, as in the case of Paul's final imprisonment (2 Tim. 4:9-11). But generally in times of difficulty, those who open their hearts to others find the fulfillment of Christ's promise that

no one who has left home or brothers or sisters or mother or father or children or fields for me and the gospel will fail to receive hundred times as much in this present age (homes, brothers, sisters, mothers, children and fields—and with them persecutions) and in the age to come, eternal life" (Mark 10:29-30).

Though the sacrifice mentioned by Christ is not exactly the same, the principle presented here, that God provides sufficient grace to face hardships, applies always in the experience of God's faithful servants. Note that Jesus says God provides us with "brothers, sisters, mothers, children." These are ties of love and commitment which are a great source of strength and comfort in times of hardship.

Jesus, of course, is realistic when he adds "and with them, persecutions." We are not immune to hardship, but the hardship provides God with an opportunity to shower on us sufficient grace. This becomes a great encouragement and incentive to firmer commitment to the way of the cross. The grace, as we said, is often mediated through fellow Christians. Thus we realize that the price for a life of sacrificial service to others is well worth paying.

The statement that God is no one's debtor is always true. We may seem deprived of some earthly comforts, like our privacy, because we chose the path of spiritual accountability to a group. But God ensures that always we have that "life . . . to the full" that Christ came to give us (John 10:10). We are fulfilled people. One way God mediates fulfillment to us is through friends, for God made us as communal beings, and therefore, community is a basic ingredient, of a fulfilled life.

People hunger for fulfillment yet look for it in the

wrong places. In fact, many people avoid the commitment true friendship requires, thinking such commitment hinders fulfillment. That is the extent to which the false philosophy of "self-fulfillment" has blinded us from seeing where true fulfillment is found.

## Strength to Defend Ourselves

Ecclesiastes 4:12 describes how friends help us when we have to defend ourselves: "Though one may be overpowered, two can defend themselves." When we are active in doing God's will, we often face attacks from hostile forces. When we have other people together with us in these battles, we are much stronger. The verse describes this strength vividly: "A cord of three strands is not quickly broken." Some of the forces we battle are earthly, others are directly satanic. We will briefly look at both these areas of battle here.

A simple illustration will help explain how friends help us in our battle against earthly forces. The missionary arm of our ministry has been doing pioneering evangelism in some Buddhist villages. People from these villages have been converted and baptized. This has been a great joy to us, but it has also opened us to attacks from people who are unhappy that others are giving up the national religion to follow another religion.

One day I got a letter from a government official challenging our actions and asking for the baptismal certificates of those baptized. He had much authority in the villages in which we were working, so I was concerned.

Before I took action, I showed the letter to my colleagues and to board members. One of them pointed out that this letter had not come on government letterhead, a fact I had not noticed. This meant it was not an official letter. Another said he knew a Christian constitutional lawyer who could give us advice. Following the lawyer's advice we decided the wisest thing to do was not to respond to the letter. There the matter ended.

Often when we are attacked, we lash out in defense without thinking too much about the consequences. These sudden reactions usually complicate matters and do not help us find a solution.

Let's look at another common occurrence. Someone criticizes a Christian leader unfairly. The leader is so upset about this that he wants to respond to the criticism immediately. He writes a letter in his defense and circulates it widely. Most of those who receive the letter do not even know of the criticism. The letter was written in such a provocative way that it creates a stir in the community. The letter does more damage to the credibility of the leader than the criticism itself. A friend would have helped him act more sensibly under fire and convinced him that making the controversy public would damage him more than help him.

Lone people often act irrationally when attacked. Out of their insecurity they lash out, perhaps in an effort to feel strong when they feel weak. They need someone who will calm them and help them to avoid irrational reactions.

The principle of the value of friends when we are under fire is applicable in many other areas of life, such as trouble in the workplace. Often when under fire in the workplace, a person's first reaction is to look for another job. Friends can suggest other options.

While Satan may be behind the attacks that come to us from human sources, he sometimes attacks in a more direct manner. Paul describes this in Ephesians 6:12. "Our struggle is not against flesh and blood, but against the rulers, against the authorities, against the powers of this dark world and against spiritual forces of evil in the heavenly realms." Paul's advises us to "put on the full armor of God, so that when the day of evil comes, you may be able to stand your ground" (6:13). He then describes the armor (6:14-18).

There is something we often overlook when we study this popular passage about spiritual warfare. The "you" does not refer to a lone soldier carrying out a war valiantly against Satan. The "you" is plural. In English "you" can be either singular or plural, and we usually think of it as being singular. But what Ephesians 6 describes is an army at war against Satan's forces. That's how God intends us to carry out our battles against demonic forces—as an army.

When we think of our battles against Satan, we usually think of temptation to personal sin. This is indeed an important aspect of our battles. But sometimes our battles may be a more direct and public confrontation with demonic forces. We face this, for example, when we minister in an area that had been under the control of demonic powers. Animistic villages in some countries and satanic cults in the West are examples of these spheres of activity. We may be called to minister to a persons who are demon possessed.

At such times of direct confrontation with Satan

and his armies, it is crucial that we not go alone. We are vulnerable to the attacks of Satan because we are directly invading his territory. He will work extra hard to defeat us. In such battles we are prone to such problems as fear, discouragement, and making hasty judgments. Friends help us overcome such problems.

It is a sad fact that many Christian workers who have battled directly with the demonic have fallen into sexual sin. This is but one example of Satan's strategy to attack those who dare to battle him.

The thrust of Ephesians 6:12-18 then is that we must not try to battle alone. If it is impossible for us to find someone to be with us when we are in a battle, God will surely provide sufficient grace. But we must always remember that this is not the norm. The norm for battling in the Christian life is in the context of a fellowship or army of believers.

Sometimes, when forced by unavoidable circumstances to battle alone, we can get others to support us in prayer. James O. Fraser was impelled against his wishes to minister alone in the mountains of China. Yet Fraser had a band of friends in his home country of England who were committed to pray for him. He faithfully kept them motivated to pray by sending regular reports of the work and discourses on the prayer he needed to cope with his challenges. *Mountain Rain,* Eileen Grossman's biography of Fraser, contains helpful hints on how to get others to join us in our battles through wrestling in prayer for us, as Epaphras did for the Colossians (Col. 4:12).

## Friendship and Personal Problems

When we have personal problems, the best people to help us are people who are close to us, like friends and relatives. Today when people have personal problems they often go to a specialist like a psychiatrist.

Thomas Szaz, himself a psychiatrist, has said that psychotherapy is the purchase of friendship. He does not mean, of course, that friends can solve all the problems people take to psychotherapists. We need specialists for extreme problems. But many problems people take to psychiatrists and other specialists might be more effectively handled by friends.

Christian psychologist Gary Collins calls this peer counseling. In his book *How to Be a People Helper*, he shows that studies have revealed that the so-called lay helper is as effective and sometimes more effective than the professional counselor. Collins suggests five advantages friends have over professionals. The peer helper

a. is closer to the helpee, knows him as a friend, and is thus better able to understand his problem and to pick up non-verbal clues or to demonstrate a sincere empathy;

b. is more often available and is thus able to provide help consistently and whenever it is especially needed;

c. often knows about the helpees family, work situation, life-style, beliefs or neighborhood and can therefore take a more active part in guiding decisions or helping the helpee to change his life situation;

d. is able to communicate in language—including slang or one's native tongue—which the helpee can easily understand; and

e. is more down-to-earth, relaxed, open, informal, and inclined to introduce a tension-relieving humor (pp. 58-59).

Yet few people are willing to spend the time needed to help a friend with a personal problem. It takes time to listen to friends share their problems, to comfort the sorrowful, and to counsel those in need of guidance. Helping friends overcome personality problems is a special challenge requiring high commitment. Because many are not willing to offer such commitment, the only recourse some people have is to go to a specialist.

Ron Lee Davis gives a good example of the power of the Christian community to act as a healing agent in his book *Gold in the Making*. Ruth, a North American, had been an active worker in her church, having served as Christian education director. But Ruth became severely depressed and had to quit her job and her work in her church. She withdrew from friendships and social contacts and took large doses of tranquilizers prescribed by her physician. She then sought help from a psychiatrist and also from her pastor.

While Ruth was in this desperate state, her pastor moved to a distant church. He decided that before he left he would do all he could to help Ruth. He visited her psychiatrist, who told him, "There is absolutely nothing we can do for Ruth. She's in a state of deep depression, and it is my opinion that she will remain in that depression for the rest of her life. No one will ever be able to help Ruth."

But the pastor did not give up on Ruth. He referred

Ruth to a house church within the congregation. Ron Davis describes this church as

> a group of eight or ten people who had committed themselves to each other to study the Bible together, to pray for each other and support each other, to be open, honest and sensitive to each other, and to hold all sharing within the group in strict confidence.

This group sought to model the type of friendship we have been describing in this book.

The group members were not told of Ruth's problems. They became her friends. Three months after joining the group, she was completely off prescribed drugs. Within six months she had returned to work. Today she is cured of her depression. Friends helped her become whole again (pp. 77-79).

## *The Pleasantness of Friends*

We have come to the end of this book! Many things have been said about friendship. The reader may have been surprised at how much Proverbs says on the topic and how relevant it is for today. We have one more text to look at. Let me simply quote the verse and express my prayer and wish that you experience the joy of having friends who are closer than a brother or sister. Proverbs 27:9 says, "Perfume and incense bring joy to the heart, and the pleasantness of one's friend springs from his earnest counsel."

# Organizational Goals and Our Personal Vision

In this book we have stressed that people should be committed to each other and their groups. But does that stifle the growth of individuals in the group? What should we do if a person in our group has a different vision than the group? How about the person who has gifts that should be used outside the group, too? In this appendix we will explore ways the principle of commitment applies in organizational life, especially in relation to the personal development and fulfillment of individual members.

Take persons who seem to have a vision different from the organization they work for. They should first share this with brothers and sisters in the group, then the group should seek to discern whether the vision is indeed of the Lord. If convinced the vision is of the Lord, the group can see whether its structure can be adjusted to accommodate the vision.

Some of the most exciting developments in our work in YFC in Sri Lanka have come in this way. God burns into the heart of one member the vision of a certain program of ministry. The leadership discusses and prays about it. They see it is something YFC can do, and they launch out. The process of deciding, of course, is not always very simple. Sometimes we agonize. Usually changes are made to the original scheme as the wisdom of the body affects it. The originator of the scheme may find this difficult to accept. Yet he or she soon realizes that the original vision is improved.

Such flexibility accommodates gifts of group members. It is not as alien to modern management thinking as it seems at first. In his autobiographical *Adventures of a Bystander*, Peter F. Drucker shows that Alfred Sloane, legendary head of General Motors, used such an approach in managing his team (pp. 256-293).

When a group shows concern and sensitivity to visions and gifts of its workers, it affirms a crucial aspect of what we may call "body theology." According to this theology, the body consists of individual members, and God has a wonderful plan for both the body and the members. Because it is God's will for the members to be in this body, then his will for the members should harmonize with his will for the body.

If persons are completely fulfilled according to God's perspective, then organizations for which they work will also be completely fulfilled. This is because God's best for the organization will include in it God's best for the member. But we are talking here about fulfillment according to God's perspective, not humanity's. For members, that may mean doing things they are not particularly adept at or fond of.

For example, a great preacher may need to write many letters and reports, visit donors to the organization or ill staff members, purchase office equipment, and do other things that seem to benefit the organization and not himself. But they *do* benefit the preacher as well. A problem in the church today is that, with specialization, people in ministry are finding it ever more difficult to integrate the various aspects of the whole counsel of God. They think it is a waste of time for a preacher to spend time visiting the sick. But such experiences give them background from which to develop sermons. Their sermons will have relevance and depth because they know how to minister to the needs of people.

Pure specialists may produce many fine materials. But the materials may lack insights needed to truly influence people in the ways of God.

Now let us consider the case of a member of an organization who may have preaching gifts that should be used outside the organization as well. The leaders of the organization, however, are not enthusiastic about this. So the member takes these speaking engagements privately without seeking approval of the leadership. He takes trips secretly. When his support team finds out, there is an unpleasant confrontation. All this contradicts the body theology of ministry.

If this member and the organization adopted the body theology approach, the first thing they would do would be to discuss this vision of a wider ministry. In fact, the initiator of the discussion might be a leader who sees that a member of the group has potential for a wider ministry. Good leaders often have ambitions for those they lead which surpass their personal ambitions. The body then agrees this is indeed a valid course of action and releases the preacher for occasional ministry outside the organization.

Now he does not need to do the ministry secretly, but with the blessing of his leaders. They proudly see his achievements as part of their outreach. The leadership helps him decide which invitations to accept and which to reject.

He, on the other hand, may decide that the honoraria given him should return to the movement. He does not say, "This is my hard-earned money," and keep it. Hardworking typists in the organization would not be able to earn such money however hard they worked. And in God's sight they are as important. In fact, they may be the ones who wrote to places where the preacher ministered and made arrangements.

The movement, in response, ensures that special expenses incurred in this itinerant ministry are met. They may see to it, for example, that he has enough money to phone his family when on the road and that he has sufficient books for study and preparation.

Does not all this hinder the success of the organization the preacher works for? After all, other organizations and churches are growing because of his input. Perhaps it hinders success if measured from a worldly standpoint, for there may be no measurable results in terms of growth of the organization. But according to kingdom thinking, the preacher *is* serving the organization, for here success is measured according to how much the *kingdom* grew because of the organization.

Missionary involvement is an important factor in assessing the success of a church or organization. But much missionary involvement does not result in measurable growth of the group, though the kingdom of God has grown. Here again, in taking management principles from the competitive marketplace, Christians have become unbiblical. Competition may be suitable for the marketplace but is heretical when applied to kingdom living, where different organizations and churches are members of the body of Christ. In the marketplace, establishments with different owners compete with each other for profits. But in God's kingdom, all establishments have the same owner—God!

We are not describing a structure with no discipline, where all can do what they want. There is exacting discipline here—the discipline of spiritual accountability. This is a bigger challenge to selfish individualism than strict organizational structure. It touches not only on those features related directly to job descriptions of members, but also on their personal lives.

We may find that job descriptions and other disciplines modern management systems advocate are useful. But these must be subject to our theology that says the group of believers is the body of Christ. Often today management systems usurp biblical body theology and take over as the supreme principle influencing the organizational life of Christian groups.

Sometimes a person's vision for ministry does not match organizational goals. If the originator really believes this path must be followed, he or she will have to leave the group. (We discussed ways this might be done in chapter 3.)

# Index of
# Principle Texts Discussed

# Commentaries and Studies on Proverbs and Ecclesiastes

Citations in this book from the commentaries are identified only by the authors name and are not footnoted. They are taken from the discussion in the commentary of the verse being studied.

Aitken, Kenneth T. *Proverbs*. The Daily Bible Study Series. Philadelphia: The Westminster Press, 1986.

Alden, Robert L. *Proverbs*. Grand Rapids: Baker Book House, 1983.

Bridges, Charles. *A Commentary on Proverbs.* Edinburgh and Carlyle: The Banner of Truth Trust, 1987 reprint of 1846 edition.

Eaton, Michael A. *Ecclesiastes*. Tyndale Old Testament Commentaries. Downers Grove, Ill.: InterVarsity Press, 1983.

Kidner, Derek. *Proverbs*. Tyndale Old Testament Commentaries. Downers Grove, Ill.: InterVarsity Press, 1964.

Martin, Charles G. "Proverbs," *The International Bible Commentary*. Edited by F. F. Bruce, et al. Grand Rapids: The Zondervan Corporation, 1986.

Scott, R. B. Y. *Proverbs. Ecclesiastes*. The Anchor Bible. Garden City, N.Y.: Doubleday and Co., 1965.

Voorwinde, Stephen. *Wisdom for Today's Issues*. Phillipsburg, N.J.: Puritan and Reformed Publishing Co., 1981.

# *Bibliography*

Bruce, F. F. *The Pauline Circle.* Exeter: Paternoster Press, and Grand Rapids: Wm. B. Eerdmans Publishing Co., 1985.

Collins, Gary. *How to Be a People Helper.* Santa Ana: Vision House Publishers, 1976.

Davis, Ron Lee. *Gold in the Making.* Nashville: Thomas Nelson Publishers, 1983.

Drucker, Peter F. *Adventures of a Bystander.* New York: Harper & Row, 1979.

France, R. T. *Matthew.* Tyndale New Testament Commentaries. Grand Rapids: William B. Eerdmans Publishing Co., 1985.

Grossman, Eileen. *Mountain Rain.* Singapore: Overseas Missionary Fellowship, 1988.

Harris, R. Laird, Gleason L. Archer, Bruce K. Waltke, eds. *Theological Wordbook of the Old Testament.* Chicago: Moody Press, 1980.

Inrig, Gary. *Quality Friendship.* Chicago: Moody Press, 1981.

Lewis, C. S. *The Four Loves.* London: Geoffrey Bles, 1960.

Morris, Leon. *Reflections on the Gospel of John.* Vol. 1. Grand Rapids: Baker Book House, 1986.

Sayer, George. *Jack: C. S. Lewis and His Times.* San Fransisco: Harper & Row, 1988.

E. D. Schmitz, "Unanimity," *The New International Dictionary of New Testament Theology.* Vol. 3. Colin Brown, ed. Grand Rapids: Zondervan Publishing House, 1978.

Yankelovich, Daniel. *New Rules: Searching for Self-fulfillment in a World Turned Upside Down.* New York: Random House, 1981.

# The Author

**A**jith Fernando has been national director of Youth for Christ (YFC) in Sri Lanka since 1976. His primary responsibility is to lead a YFC team he has been part of for over twenty-five years.

Following schooling in Colombo (Sri Lanka), he received a B.S. in biology from Vidyalankara University of Ceylon (Sri Lanka). In 1974 he received an M.Div. from Asbury Theological Seminary (Kentucky) and in 1989 was awarded Asbury's Distinguished Alumnus Award. He received a Th.M. in New Testament from Fuller Theological Seminary (California) in 1976. In 1988 he was visiting professor of missions at Gordon-Conwell Theological Seminary (Massachusetts), which gave him an honorary doctor of divinity degree.

Under the influence of his mother, a convert from

Buddhism, Ajith committed his life to Christ during his teen years. In 1980, Ajith and his wife, Nelun, started and currently help lead a Sinhala speaking congregation at the Nugegoda Methodist church in Sri Lanka. Nugegoda members are primarily converts from Buddhism and Hinduism.

Ajith's concern for evangelism and leadership development among the economically poor is expressed in most aspects of his life and ministry. The YFC ministry in Sri Lanka has pioneered development of culturally relevant youth evangelism models.

Ajith has written several books in English and Sinhala. He also serves as a principle translator of the Sinhala Living Bible.

His work outside Sri Lanka takes him to settings such as the Urbana conferences to do Bible expositions. He serves on the Lausanne Committee for World Evangelization. He has been chair of two Urbana-like missions conferences in Sri Lanka—Navodaya 88 and Navodaya 92.

When not traveling, Ajith lives in Colombo, Sri Lanka, with Nelun and his daughter, Nirmali, (1980) and son, Asiri (1983).